Old Whigs

Old Whigs

Burke, Lincoln,
and the
Politics of Prudence

Greg Weiner

Encounter
BOOKS

New York • London

First American edition published in 2019 by Encounter Books,
an activity of Encounter for Culture and Education, Inc.,
a nonprofit, tax-exempt corporation.
Encounter Books website address: www.encounterbooks.com

Manufactured in the United States and printed on
acid-free paper. The paper used in this publication meets
the minimum requirements of ANSI/NISO Z39.48–1992
(R 1997) (*Permanence of Paper*).

FIRST AMERICAN EDITION

LIBRARY OF CONGRESS CATALOGING-IN-PUBLICATION DATA
Names: Weiner, Greg, author.
Title: Old Whigs : Burke, Lincoln, and the politics of prudence /
by Greg Weiner.
Description: New York : Encounter Books, [2019] |
Includes bibliographical references and index.
Identifiers: LCCN 2018053320 (print) | LCCN 2019010769 (ebook) |
ISBN 9781641770514 (ebook) | ISBN 9781641770507 (hardcover : alk. paper)
Subjects: LCSH: Political leadership—Moral and ethical aspects. |
Prudence—Political aspects. | Burke, Edmund, 1729–1797—Political and
social views. | Lincoln, Abraham, 1809–1865—Political and social views. |
Whig Party (Great Britain)—History. | Whig Party (U.S.)—History. |
Political science—Great Britain—History—18th century. | United
States—Politics and government—19th century.
Classification: LCC JC330.3 (ebook) | LCC JC330.3 .W45 2019 (print) |
DDC 172—dc23
LC record available at https://lccn.loc.gov/2018053320

"But the reason why things are ordained to their end is, properly speaking, providence, because it is the principal part of prudence. The other two parts of prudence, memory of the past and understanding of the present, are subordinate to it, helping us to decide how to provide for the future."

—St. Thomas Aquinas, *Summa Theologica*

"A disposition to preserve, and an ability to improve, taken together, would be my standard of a statesman."

—Burke, *Reflections on the Revolution in France*

"And now, beware of rashness. Beware of rashness, but with energy, and sleepless vigilance, go forward, and give us victories."

—Lincoln to General Joseph Hooker, January 26, 1863

Dedication

For my parents

CONTENTS

Acknowledgments

In this as in all such undertakings, I have incurred substantial debts, intellectual and personal alike. At some point I will make an honest writer of myself and give my Assumption College colleague Daniel J. Mahoney a co-author credit on everything I write. His intellectual partnership is that integral; my only hesitation is imputing responsibility to him for my errors. Daniel P. Maher of Assumption's Department of Philosophy has also been generous with his time and insight as a guide to Aristotle and far more. Marc Guerra of the College's Department of Theology has tutored me in Aquinas and classical prudence, among other topics. The College also provided me with a sabbatical during which I undertook research for this project, for which I am indebted to its president, Francesco Cesareo, and its provost, Louise Carroll Keeley. To my other colleagues in political science, Bernard J. Dobski, Jeremy Geddert, Deborah O'Malley, and Geoffrey Vaughan, I am grateful for conversation and collegiality that far exceed what friends at other institutions report is available to them. I am also grateful to Yuval Levin for conversation and counsel on Burke. Errors are, of course, my own.

Roger Kimball of Encounter Books saw promise in this project. I am deeply thankful to him and to his editorial team for that and for their consummate skill in bringing it to fruition.

As I write these words on a Sunday afternoon, my family—my wife, Rebecca, and my children, Hannah, Jacob, and Theodore—are once more tolerating my absence, absent-mindedness, or both. More than that patience, I am grateful for their examples of relentless inquiry, prudence, and moral imagination.

Introduction

Edmund Burke was convinced the Jacobins were coming for his bones.

He had been unrelenting in his opposition to the French Revolution, resisting peace talks with the Directory even when its march across Europe and, perhaps, the sceptered isle itself seemed inexorable. By the time of his death, Burke, seeing Jacobinism victorious abroad and teeming at home, had asked to be buried in an unmarked grave lest the revolutionaries desecrate his remains. His resting place is unknown to this day. The great modern theorist of prudence had, if we interpret the term simplistically, been singularly imprudent—which is to say incautious—in this as in other projects: defending the rights of the American colonists; his similarly controversial advocacy on behalf of Irish Catholics; his years-long and doomed prosecution of Warren Hastings, the brutal and corrupt governor-general of India.

Abraham Lincoln, too, spurned caution insofar as we understand that term to mean a disposition to surrender to long odds. He insisted on union, believing in victory even after calamities early in the Civil War made it seem untenable. He refused to suspend the 1864 presidential election even when, as late as August of that year, it appeared he would lose and the White House would fall to the accommodationist Democrat and spurned general George B. McClellan. Even in the moment of triumph, Lincoln's Second Inaugural declared that North and South shared blame for the torrents of blood.

Yet both Burke and Lincoln, this study argues, are best understood as prudent statesmen. In the entire political lexicon, perhaps no term is deployed at a higher ratio of use to understanding. President George H. W. Bush was pilloried for his frequent refrain that a course of action "wouldn't be prudent." The term connotes caution, to the point of timidity to some and cowardice to others. Yet this is to misunderstand prudence as a classical virtue, one for whose recovery contemporary politics aches. Genuine prudence entails what Burke called "a moral rather than a complexional timidity." Prudence is cautious not out of fear—what he also called "a false, reptile prudence"—but rather from a moral commitment to the limits of individual reason. At the same time, there are moments when prudence demands bold action and unbending tenacity. The key to prudence is knowing the difference, having the capacity of judgment that can distinguish between ordinary moments and genuine crises and, in either case, calibrating action to proper goals.

Burke and Lincoln are odd partners in such a conversation even if, as the Burke scholar Jesse Norman argues, Lincoln's leadership was "Burkean through and through." There is no evidence that Lincoln read Burke or was influenced by him—Norman notes that there is, by contrast, ample evidence that Lincoln read Burke's rival Thomas Paine—and the word "prudence" appears only a handful of times in Lincoln's writings. Even then, he generally associated it with caution, as in his first annual message to Congress in December 1861, when he said he had enforced confiscation laws according to "the dictates of prudence, as well as the obligations of law...." While both men climbed from modest circumstances to the heights of statesmanship, Burke cut an elegant rhetorical path through some of the greatest controversies of his day. What Burke said of Marie Antoinette—that she hardly seemed to touch the earth—might be said of his prose. Lincoln, by contrast, was a rough-hewn backwoods lawyer whose mature rhetoric, while eloquent, is characterized by an unmistakable heaviness. Burke was a famed skeptic of the French dogma of universal human rights; Lincoln, like Burke an opponent of slavery, spoke frequently in the idiom of equality and liberty.

Yet there is an intriguing connection. Burke and Lincoln both described themselves as "old Whigs," a reference in Burke's case to the party that opposed the power of the royal court in favor of Parliament and in Lincoln's to the party that stood against the populist demagoguery of President Andrew Jackson. There are many differences between the British and American Whig experiences, but prudence links them. Burke wrote in his *Appeal from the New to the Old Whigs* that "they who go with the principles of the ancient Whigs, which are those contained in [*Reflections on the Revolution in France*], never can go too far.... The opinions maintained in that book never can lead to an extreme, because their foundation is laid in an opposition to extremes." In his 1854 Peoria Address, Lincoln sought to correct Whigs who feared being cast as radicals if they supported restoring the Missouri Compromise. "Will they allow me as an old whig to tell them good humoredly, that I think this is very silly? Stand with anybody that stands RIGHT. Stand with him while he is right and PART with him when he goes wrong.... In both cases you oppose the dangerous extremes."

In his *The Ethics of Rhetoric*, Richard Weaver, who places Burke and Lincoln in a conversation about methods of rhetorical reasoning, also notices this connection, but chiefly by way of criticism of Burke. For Weaver, Whiggism in both the British and American experiences was defined by opposition and circumstantial reasoning rather than innate principle. Lincoln, Weaver claims, had to leave the aimless Whig Party and join the principled Republicans for his greatness to emerge. But this is to mistake the status of prudence as a virtue and the rooting, for both men, of moderation in moral soil. Both British and American Whigs *were* principled, most obviously in their opposition to executive power. But prudence is also a principle, as is circumstantial reasoning. Both are based on the objectively moral idea that there are limits to human reason.

Placing the reflections of these "Old Whigs" in relief thus helps to illuminate prudence in its full dimensions: inflected with caution but not confined to it, bound to circumstances, and finding expression in the particular yet grounded in the absolute. These dimensions point toward a recovery of prudence as the political virtue *par excellence*. Today is an era of American, perhaps of global, politics in which all positions are stated in extremes, even when they are crafted in moderation. All conflicts seem ultimate, every election a choice between redemption and doom. Some issues are ultimate, of course, and there are likewise forks in historical roads at which one path leads to constitutional health and the other to national calamity. These are rare, they require resolve, and even as prudence counsels us to beware the rhetoric of catastrophe, it demands that we recognize emergencies when we confront them.

But exigencies must be addressed, and moral absolutes pursued, prudently too. Burke's warning that "moderation will be stigmatized as the virtue of cowards; and compromise as the prudence of traitors" is a prophecy for our time, and neither party is immune. We fear tolerating enemies either to the left or the right precisely because we lack prudence. That is not to endorse a geographic or geometrical centrism according to which political virtue lies evenly between whatever the partisan edges happen to be at a given time. Burke's moderation was anchored in moral soil and intellectual humility. Prudence refuses to believe that any individual at any moment has discovered the solutions to all political problems. Such confidence in reason is the road to utopian disaster: the essence of Jacobinism. Moderation was an absolute in a dual sense: The necessity for it arose from a morally objective humility as well as an intellectual recognition of the variability of circumstances, and the use of it was invariably in pursuit of morally objective ends.

So it was for Lincoln. He experimented with scheme after scheme for gradual and compensated emancipation before issuing his famous proclamation in the face of military necessity. His much-misunderstood opposition to the Kansas-Nebraska Act was not merely the product of moral revulsion at the expansion of slavery—a topic on which he meticulously sought to elevate public opinion over time—but also political caution about repealing the Missouri Compromise *as a compromise.* If this great measure was repealed, no one would ever trust in such a mechanism of accommodation and moderation again. If the Kansas-Nebraska Act stood, Lincoln declared at Peoria, "we shall have repudiated—discarded from the councils of the Nation—the SPIRIT OF COMPROMISE; for who after this will ever trust a national compromise? The spirit of mutual concession—that spirit which first gave us the constitution, and which has thrice saved the Union—we shall have strangled and cast from us forever."

This is prudent accommodation, embraced not from fear but rather for principle. The risk is that prudence becomes tautological, a proposition that cannot be refuted: The right course is prudent, the wrong imprudent; boldness is prudent when boldness is required, caution is prudent in more appropriately cautious circumstances. The issue is complicated by the clarity of retrospection, made all the more ironic because foresight is so characteristic of prudence. But it is inescapably easier to see Lincoln's prudence a century and a half after the Union triumph than it was in the morose days following Bull Run. Similarly, the Terror eventually vindicated Burke's early warnings about where the French Revolution was headed, but the courage required for a Whig to oppose rebellion against an absolute crown immediately upon the Bastille's fall was immense. Yet retrospection may be the quality prudence values most: We discover and instantiate objective values in the theater of history, where principle plays out on the stage of infinitely variable circumstance. Burke wrote in his *Thoughts on the Cause of the Present Discontents* that "retrospective wisdom, and historical patriotism, are things of wonderful convenience, and serve admirably to reconcile the old quarrel between speculation and practice."

A similar risk inheres in imputing a mystical character to prudence, reducing it to a quality of intuition and judgment that some statesmen innately possess and others lack. There is some of that, to be sure: Certain dispositions are more given to prudence than others, and some actors on the public stage have an uncanny capacity to intuit the unfolding of events. But leaving prudence to such contingencies is itself imprudent. Prudence is more art than science. One of Burke's central teachings is that politics cannot be reduced to arithmetic or geometrical precision, while one of the aspects of Lincoln's political genius was his ability to mask—perhaps to ground—his capacity of judgment, informed by a study of history, in the guise of a country bumpkin lawyer. Yet that does not mean the quality of judgment cannot be cultivated and encouraged, especially if we make an active effort to understand what prudence means and, crucially, if we do so not in the abstract but rather through the eyes of two of its exemplars.

What we shall see in the pages that follow is that prudence involves a carefully choreographed dance between principle and circumstance, what Burke called "a moral prudence and discretion, the general principles of which never vary...." Principle is the end according to which prudence decides on its courses. Burke thus wrote to Dr. William Markham in 1771 that he had not learned principles from history, but he had learned prudence—how to attain principles—from it. "My principles enable me to form my judgment upon Men and Actions in History, just as they do in current life; and are not formed out of events and Characters, either present or past. History is a preceptor of Prudence not of principles." Significantly, he explained in his 1793 "Remarks on the Policy of the Allies with Respect to France," history "improve[d] the understanding, by showing both men and affairs in a great variety of views. From this source much political wisdom may be learned,—that is, may be learned as habit, not as precept." His specific meaning was that history did not furnish casuistic "cases and precedents for a lawyer." It could inculcate prudence as a disposition and capacity for judgment, not provide debating points for rhetoricians.

Prudence requires the use of reason, but also humility about its limits. It entails a capacity to distinguish between the ordinary and the urgent. Burke wrote in the *Reflections*: "In history a great volume is unrolled for our instruction, drawing the materials of future wisdom from the past errors and infirmities of mankind." We might also draw the materials of future wisdom from two old Whigs who exemplified caution and boldness, who valued reason but applied it to circumstance, and who found the needs of the present and the shape of the future along the road of the past. That future wisdom is the very definition of prudence.

To recover it, we must return, in the fashion of Burke and Lincoln, to first principles. For Aristotle, prudence—*phronēsis*, sometimes rendered as "practical wisdom"—referred to the capacity to choose the right means for attaining the worthy ends. In his *Ethics,* Aristotle explains that truth is attained by art, science, prudence, wisdom, and intellect. Prudence is the capacity of deliberating on things that could be otherwise. "It seems to belong to a prudent person to be able to deliberate nobly about things good and advantageous for himself, not in a partial way—for example, the sorts of things conducive to health or to strength—but about the sorts of things conducive to living well in general." Prudence belongs specifically to a realm of "action"; it thus differs from "art," which pertains to "making," and "science," which deals with the unalterable and precise. It is not as precise as either of these endeavors. Thus, "prudence is a true characteristic that is bound up with action, accompanied by reason, and concerned with things good and bad for a human being."

True prudence, as distinguished from what Aristotle calls "mere cunning," is oriented toward right ends. "[P]rudence is necessarily a characteristic accompanied by reason, in possession of the truth, and bound up with action pertaining to the human goods," Aristotle teaches. It is not merely the capacity to choose the best means to morally neutral goods: "If…the target is a noble one, the cleverness is praiseworthy; but if base, it is mere cunning."

Political prudence is a capacity some people seem innately to possess, but one that is sharpened by experience. Aristotle therefore remarks that young people are "wise" in geometry and mathematics, "but a young person does not seem to be prudent. The cause is that prudence is also of particulars, which come to be known as a result of experience, but a young person is inexperienced: a long period of time creates experience."

Two concepts are latent here. One is that prudence, being a realm of action, depends on particulars. We experience the universal through the particular. Second, one acquires an understanding of these particulars by experiencing them over a long period of time, just as Burke had written that political prudence was "not to be taught a priori. Nor is it a short experience that can instruct us in that practical science...." Crucially, for Aristotle, prudent deliberation is not "good guesswork." The reason is instructive. Good guesswork is "unaccompanied by reasoned argument and something swift, whereas people deliberate for a long time and assert that while they ought to do swiftly what has been deliberated about, they ought to deliberate slowly." In Aristotle's *Politics*, prudence is the virtue uniquely associated with the ruler as opposed to the citizen. In a similar way, Burke's *Letters on a Regicide Peace* declined to identify prudence with guesswork, instead associating it, suggestively, with "rules": "It would not be pious error, but mad and impious presumption, for any one to trust in an unknown order of dispensations, in defiance of the rules of prudence, which are formed upon the known march of the ordinary providence of God."

This superintending concept of providence constitutes Aquinas's addition to Aristotelian prudence, one of the cardinal Thomist virtues. Providence is, for Aquinas, "the principal part of prudence." Providence is "the reason why things are ordained to their end...." Prudence is the virtue associated with reason. It has, in this sense, a deeply normative cast, which is to say that the point of prudence is not what Aristotle calls "cunning." It guides reason, one part of which must be knowing reason's limits. For Aquinas, as for Aristotle, prudence requires habit arising from long experience. Aquinas does not equate prudence with Burke's "moral timidity," but he does oppose it to "temerity." Prudence is the chief of the moral virtues because it "attains reason through itself."

The *Oxford English Dictionary* lists uses of prudence that associate it with such virtues as "temperance" and "patience" as early as the fifteenth century. But as Chapter 1 will endeavor to show, it was not until Burke that it was fully theorized as such. Aristotelian and Thomist prudence includes caution, but not necessarily so: Caution is prudent if it is the best means of attaining good ends, but it is not inherently so, a point evident in Burke's evocative reference in notes for parliamentary debate on America to "an exalted principle, and...an heroic prudence, which are not the less just and true, but the more true and the more just, because they are nearer to the correct standard of a perfect nature, and not muddled and concocted with the dregs of mean passions and little views." For Alexis de Tocqueville, it has more of the connotation of caution: In *The Old Regime and the French Revolution,* the late Bourbon monarchy, lacking ample means of coercion, "had to grope its way, so to speak, in the dark and exercise much prudence." Tocqueville's *Recollections* on the 1848 revolution include the reflection that "all parties made great efforts of prudence and patience to prevent or at least delay the crisis." In *Democracy in America,* he equates the "prudence" of the wealthy with an erosion of ambition for towering achievement.

Tocqueville's most seasoned and mature reflection on the topic—one that evokes Aristotle and Aquinas—is his 1852 speech to the Academy of Moral and Political Sciences. There, Tocqueville says the "science" and "art" of government are different. The art of government sounds much like classical prudence. The science, "founded on the very nature of man…teaches us what laws are best adapted to the general and permanent condition of humanity." Practitioners of this science of politics resemble Burke's metaphysical politicians: They are capable when it comes to writing and analysis, but, importantly, Tocqueville writes, this very habit "enslaves them to the logic of ideas, when the crowd never obeys any logic save that of the passions." Scientific politics is associated for Tocqueville with both "monuments" and "ruins." It "produced" the French Revolution. If fully applied, a utopianism that is anathema to prudence inheres in scientific politics. Yet that does not mean prudence is not oriented toward principle. On Aristotelian and Thomist premises, it must be. Tocqueville thus said that only "barbarians…recognize in politics nothing but practice."

Tocqueville plainly means to admire the science of politics—what Burke might call philosophic politics—but must strain to do so. He cautions the Academy that its assembled members constitute "a learned society and not a political body," one that must remain "in the serene region of pure theory and abstract science." The ability to succeed in either science or art is no guarantee of skill in the other. "[I]t is even permitted to say that to make fine books, even on politics or things connected to it, prepares one quite poorly for the government of men and the management of affairs."

Winston Churchill supplies a more recent illustration of prudent statesmanship. Churchill opened his history of the Second World War by noting that the conflict could have been averted "by steadfastness in righteous convictions, and by reasonable common sense and prudence," while, on the other hand, "the counsels of prudence and restraint may become the prime agents of mortal danger [and] the middle course adopted from desires for safety and a quiet life may be found to lead direct to the bull's-eye of disaster." It bears emphasis *why* the middle course is mistakenly adopted here: not from caution or intellectual humility, but rather out of a deluded desire for "safety and a quiet life."

Churchill was not opposed to moderation in the sense in which Burke and Lincoln had counseled it, as avoiding dangerous extremes. But his eternal fame lies in perceiving that Britain in the 1930s, like America in the 1860s, faced an existential crisis in which ultimate values were at stake and in which compromise with evil was not only wrong but also imprudent. It will not do to say that Lord Halifax, Churchill's rival and foreign secretary who demanded peace negotiations as the Nazis marched across France, seemed prudent at the time. This is what Burke calls a "false, reptile prudence," and, rightly understood, it is decidedly imprudent. Churchill—a student of prudent statesmanship in his prewar writings, especially his *Life of Marlborough*—did not make an idol of daring for daring's sake. The moment—which is to say the circumstances—demanded it.

Indeed, to say that prudence always counsels caution or, for that matter, that it always demands bold action would be to violate two of Burke's most important dicta: always to consider an abstraction according to its consequences, and never to reason from the extreme to the ordinary case. Lincoln similarly understood that rebellion imparted extraordinary executive powers, but only from the necessity of the particular conditions—for example, Congress could not be quickly called into session to suspend habeas corpus or authorize a blockade of the rebellious states—and only for its duration. Like Burke and Churchill, Lincoln recognized union as an ultimate value on which compromise was imprudent because it would lead to a process of infinite division: Disaffected subdivisions would be empowered to secede from the seceded states, and other subdivisions from them in turn, such that the idea of secession was, he said in his First Inaugural, "the essence of anarchy." An essential element of prudence is thus recognizing the difference between genuine emergency and the aggrandizing rhetoric of catastrophe. Not every moment is Munich, but Munich was. A wide range of experience and circumstances is necessary to discern the difference.

There is an excellence in this kind of prudence that requires discipline, restraint, courage, and a rich appreciation of the variegation of political life. The excellence consists in several dimensions that we shall trace through the thought of Burke and Lincoln. First, the prudent statesman is committed to immovable principles but applies the faculty of prudence to choose the appropriate means of attaining them. This will sometimes require boldness, but even in boldness, it will entail modesty too. These are not incompatible: Aristotle listed both greatness of soul and prudence among the virtues. Similarly, prudence is rooted in the concrete rather than the abstract, which serves as a shield against utopian fancies. Third, prudence is confident in its aims but diffident about the power of individual reason. As a result, it relies on the accumulated wisdom of tradition.

We begin with Burke's concept of prudence, against which we shall consider Lincoln's before turning to specific respects in which the virtue played out in both men's thought.

CHAPTER ONE

෩ ෬

The God of
This Lower World

Burke on Prudence

E arly in his literary career, Burke embarked on what he planned to publish as a history of England from ancient through modern times. Much overlooked in the literature on Burke, the tens of thousands of words he completed provide compelling portraits of both prudent and imprudent statesmen, especially in the period during and immediately following the Norman Conquest. The study reads like a Burkean version of Machiavelli's *Discourses on Livy,* seeking lessons in history oriented toward fixed ideals. William the Conqueror, for example, executed "the grandeur of [his] plans" with "courage and wisdom." Yet he was also, the reader learns, "unlearned in books" and so "formed his understanding by the rigid discipline of a large and complicated experience." This is a common feature of the prudent mind, which must be "enlarged" and enriched by exposure to the variegation of human circumstances.

It was political prudence and not personal virtue with which Burke was primarily concerned. These were not wholly separable, but neither were they necessarily equivalent. Burke admired personal virtue, but he also understood that a statesman must be judged by the prudence of his public acts. Personal virtue may in fact lead to political imprudence. Burke wrote to William Markham that principle was morality enlarged. It was a virtue of personal life. Prudence, by contrast, was a political virtue that invariably involved choices. It is consequently significant that Burke attributed personal virtue but not political prudence to some of England's leading early characters.

William's eldest son, Robert, for example, was known for admirable moral qualities of a personal nature but not, Burke wrote, "that steady prudence which is necessary when the short career we are to run will not allow us to make many mistakes." Robert guided himself "solely by the impulses of an unbounded and irregular spirit." He was "vehement in his pursuits, but inconstant...." This immoderation and unsteadiness are hallmarks of imprudence. By contrast, Robert's brother William, one of the Conqueror's other sons, was wholly unvirtuous personally but "circumspect, steady, and courageous for his ends, not for glory. These qualities secured to him that fortune which the virtues of Robert deserved."

There is a taste of prudence in this account of the younger William, understood as the ability to be both "circumspect" and "steady"—note that these qualities are compatible and even complementary—in pursuit of ends, but it is not genuine, classical prudence because the ends are morally vapid. William, upon assuming the crown as William II, wisely pledged his support to the clergy as well as to ancient English liberties. Yet William's prudence deserted him when he chose an advisor, Flambard, who "inflamed all the king's passions, and encouraged him in his unjust enterprises." Upon his death in a freak hunting accident, William ultimately seemed to lack prudence or, more precisely, the ability to identify right ends. He operated against the temperament of his people without, crucially, "any great end of government...." William supplies an instance of what Aquinas called "false prudence," a capacity for cunning but not the wisdom to choose right ends toward which to orient it.

These princes' travails suggest several dimensions of prudence. Perhaps the most consistent theme is that prudence sometimes requires caution but other times requires boldness and fortitude, a need accentuated in early English history by the fact that the statesmen in question were endeavoring to establish a royal line. For this reason, prudence entails a combination of "circumspection" and "courage." We are tempted to see these qualities as at odds, but Burke suggested that the prudent statesman needed both so that each was available for the appropriate circumstance. Finally, prudence entails moderation and limitation: thus Burke's reference to Robert's "unbounded and irregular spirit." This value of limitation, as we shall see, arises from respect for the complexity of society and the boundaries of reason, the result of which was that many, if not most, political choices were between evils rather than between goods.

"Heroic Virtue"

Perhaps the single most perplexing dimension of prudence is discerning when it counsels caution and when it demands bold action. Burke's judgment, applied to changing situations on the ground, led him alternately to both conclusions. We begin with his theory of caution, one of Burke's most important contributions to the Western understanding of prudence. He was perhaps the first commentator fully to theorize the case for caution as a sort of default position rooted in the moral virtue of humility. The case was elucidated most fully in *Reflections on the Revolution in France,* Burke's 1790 broadside against the French Revolution, in which he saw with astonishing prescience that the situation in France would career out of control. The revolutionaries were, among other sins, intoxicated by reason. By contrast:

> A politic caution, a guarded circumspection, a moral rather than a complexional timidity, were among the ruling principles of our forefathers in their most decided conduct. Not being illuminated with the light of which the gentlemen of France tell us they have got so abundant a share, they acted under a strong impression of the ignorance and fallibility of mankind. He that had made them thus fallible rewarded them for having in their conduct attended to their nature.

A great deal is latent in this passage. A "complexional" timidity describes the personality of a statesman dominated by either fear of the unknown or a preference for the easy path. "Moral timidity," on the other hand, denotes prudence. It is moral because it is grounded in an understanding of human fallibility, which the French revolutionaries, convinced they were "illuminated" by wisdom unavailable to their ancestors, lacked. Moreover, this prudence has a transcendent dimension: God makes man fallible and rewards him for understanding his limits. This distinction between caution grounded in moral principle and caution arising from cowardice is central to the statesman's capacity to distinguish between situations that require assertive action and those to which reserve is more appropriate. In a 1792 letter to the Whig statesman Lord Grenville, Burke denied an "abstract principle" that prevented England from interfering in the internal affairs of Revolutionary France. The question was one of prudence understood in tandem with circumspection: "To interfere in such dissensions requires great prudence and circumspection, and a serious attention to justice and to the policy of one's own Country, as well as that of Europe."

One had to distinguish between timidity with respect to oneself and timidity with respect to political life. The former could be cowardice, whereas the latter was virtuous. In the 1770s, the American colonies found an ally in Burke, who spoke powerfully in Parliament on their behalf. His "Speech on American Taxation," which denied the prudence if not the right of the mother country of taxing the colonies, dealt with the repeal of the Townshend Act, which had been so odious to the American colonists because it attempted to raise money from them without their consent. Burke denied that the repeal of the Act in the face of a ferocious American response arose from timidity: "If, Sir, the conduct of ministry, in proposing the repeal, had arisen from timidity *with regard to themselves*, it would have been greatly to be condemned. Interested timidity disgraces as much in the cabinet as personal timidity does in the field. But timidity *with regard to the well-being of our country* is heroic virtue" (emphasis added). It was heroic precisely because it required courage in the face of accusations of cowardice.

In 1791's *Appeal from the New to the Old Whigs*, a defense of the consistency of his positions in favor of the American colonists but against the French Revolution, Burke wrote of the caution owed when risking political institutions to which future generations are the heirs: "Perhaps the only moral trust with any certainty in our hands is the care of our own time. With regard to futurity, we are to treat it like a ward. We are not so to attempt an improvement of his fortune as to put the capital of his estate to any hazard." The complexity of the British constitution places it, he wrote in the 1770 pamphlet *Thoughts on the Cause of the Present Discontents*, "on a nice equipoise, with steep precipices and deep waters upon all sides of it," such that tipping it to one side may upset its balance.

"Every project of a material change in a government so complicated as ours, combined at the same time with external circumstances still more complicated, is a matter full of difficulties; in which a considerate man will not be too ready to decide; a prudent man too ready to undertake; or an honest man too ready to promise." A decade later, writing to a county meeting in Buckinghamshire, Burke opposed radical constitutional reform on the grounds that the British regime was complex and had to be viewed as a balanced whole. "For that which taken singly and by itself may appear to be wrong, when considered with relation to other things, may be perfectly right,—or at least such as ought to be patiently endured, as the means of preventing something that is worse." That was true with respect to diagnosing constitutional ailments. "As to the *remedy* of that distemper an equal caution ought to be used; because this latter consideration is not single and separate, no more than the former.... Please God, I will walk with caution whenever I am not able clearly to see my way before me."

There is a difference, Burke suggested, between risking our own political fortunes and those of others, especially future generations'. The gradual evolution of the British constitution, he said in a 1782 parliamentary speech, "is a subject of prudent and honest use and thankful enjoyment, and not of captious criticism and rash experiment." Likewise, speaking to conciliation with the American colonies: "In every arduous enterprise, we consider what we are to lose, as well as what we are to gain; and the more and better stake of liberty every people possess, the less they will hazard in a vain attempt to make it more. These are *the cords of man*. Man acts from adequate motives relative to his interest, and not on metaphysical speculations."

Burke made a related point in one of the most celebrated and eloquent passages of the *Reflections*:

> Society is, indeed, a contract. Subordinate contracts for objects of mere occasional interest may be dissolved at pleasure; but the state ought not to be considered as nothing better than a partnership agreement in a trade of pepper and coffee, calico or tobacco, or some other such low concern, to be taken up for a little temporary interest, and to be dissolved by the fancy of the parties. It is to be looked on with other reverence; because it is not a partnership in things subservient only to the gross animal existence of a temporary and perishable nature. It is a partnership in all

science, a partnership in all art, a partnership in every virtue and in all perfection. As the ends of such a partnership cannot be obtained in many generations, it becomes a partnership not only between those who are living, but between those who are living, those who are dead, and those who are to be born.

In this passage, prudence is directed toward the ends of society, those things for which it is a partnership: science, art, virtue, and perfection. Those ends, and thus this partnership, transcend generations. Burke's notion of the current generation being "wards" for ancestry and posterity alike meant, according to the *Reflections,* that "the temporary possessors and life-renters in [the commonwealth], unmindful of what they have received from their ancestors, or of what is due to their posterity," could not "act as if they were the entire masters; [they] should not think it amongst their rights to cut off the entail or commit waste on the inheritance, by destroying at their pleasure the whole original fabric of their society...."

This, again, was a matter of moral humility: Generational wisdom exceeded individual reason. Addressing Parliament in 1775 on his plan to conciliate the American colonies by restoring their autonomy, Burke declared:

> In forming a plan for this purpose, I endeavored to put myself in that frame of mind which was the most natural and the most reasonable, and which was certainly the most probable means of securing me from all error. I set out with a perfect distrust of my own abilities, a total renunciation of every speculation of my own, and with a profound reverence for the wisdom of our ancestors, who have left us the inheritance of so happy a Constitution and so flourishing an empire, and, what is a thousand times more valuable, the treasury of the maxims and principles which formed the one and obtained the other.

We shall encounter Burke's views of tradition more fully in Chapter 7. What is important for now is that Burke was personally humble in formulating his plan but bold in advocating it. The reason for his humility—the prudent course that would save him from error—was a reluctance to trust his own capacity, as an individual exempted from the continuous chain of human wisdom, to solve the problem of American policy.

In his 1777 "Letter to the Sheriffs of Bristol," written to defend his positions on America, Burke spoke of his "incapacity" for abstract philosophical inquiry, drawing a principle of action from it: "I never shall be ashamed to confess, that, where I am ignorant, I am diffident." He separately warned constituents in Bristol against measuring what was necessary policy in Ireland according to what they wanted necessity to be. The contrast he drew is instructive: "Moderation, prudence, and equity are far more suitable to our condition than loftiness, and confidence, and rigor." In this series, "prudence" is opposed to "confidence," by which Burke meant an excessive confidence in our own capacity. Prudence was rooted in humility.

"A False, Reptile Prudence"

Yet there was also a misguided prudence that chose caution in circumstances that did not warrant it or from motives of cowardice rather than humility. In his *Letters on a Regicide Peace*, Burke excoriated legislators who refused to condemn the French Revolution because they feared the political repercussions of doing so: "If ministers, instead of following the great indications of the Constitution, proceed on such reports, they will take the whispers of a cabal for the voice of the people, and the counsels of imprudent timidity for the wisdom of a nation." This "imprudent timidity" was a personal quality that Burke opposed to "the wisdom of a nation."

The same text also called forth a national spirit that "will hearten the timidity and fix the irresolution of hesitating prudence...." This hesitating prudence recalls Prince Robert's weakness of will. What, then, is the difference between laudable and unworthy hesitation? *Regicide Peace* draws the distinction: "There is a courageous wisdom: there is also a false, reptile prudence, the result, not of caution, but of fear." Wisdom can be courageous, and fear can be imprudent. The difference appears to be the motive from which it arises and the stakes of the issue to which it is applied. Caution, in either case, is admirable in the formulation of plans, whereas fear is to be condemned. A comparable difference obtains, Burke wrote in 1791, between "rash, ill-chosen, or ill-combined" measures that result from "blind terror" rather than "enlightened foresight." Yet we must take care not to dismiss boldness as rashness. The opposite is often true, *Regicide Peace* argued: "Peace may be made as unadvisedly as war.

Nothing is so rash as fear; and the counsels of pusillanimity very rarely put off, whilst they are always sure to aggravate, the evils from which they would fly."

Jacobins were evil and Britain should expect them to act accordingly, Burke warned in his 1791 "Letter to a Member of the National Assembly." Consequently, ministers of state should act "with promptitude, decision, and steadiness on that belief." This was a matter of prudence, especially given the proximity of Jacobin France to constitutional England. "When all these circumstances combine, or the important parts of them, the duty of the vicinity calls for the exercise of its competence: and the rules of prudence do not restrain, but demand it," he wrote in *Regicide Peace*. Ministers should not "fear a responsibility for acts of manly adventure. The responsibility which they are to dread is lest they should show themselves unequal to the expectation of a brave people." In 1794, an address of the French Revolutionary moderate Jacques-Pierre Brissot was printed in pamphlet form. Burke wrote a preface in which he described Jacobinism as an ultimate issue on which compromise was imprudent:

> In a cause like this, and in a time like the present, there is no neutrality. They who are not actively, and with decision and energy, against Jacobinism are its partisans. They who do not dread it love it. It cannot be viewed with indifference. It is a thing made to produce a powerful impression on the feelings. Such is the nature of Jacobinism, such is the nature of man, that this system must be regarded either with enthusiastic admiration, or with the highest degree of detestation, resentment, and horror.

Again differentiating between caution in choosing a course and boldness in executing it, Burke wrote to Rockingham in 1777 of the American revolt: "To pursue violent measures with languor and irresolution, is not very consistent in speculation, and not more reputable or safe in practice....[I]f they do not undertake [war] with a certain degree of zeal, and even with warmth and indignation, it had better be removed wholly out of our thoughts." Such irresolution was logically inconsistent; in practice, though, what made boldness prudent was that languor was not "safe." For this reason, it was important to recognize which issues were ultimate and to adjust one's actions to that ranking:

"Too great a sense of the value of a subordinate interest may be the very source of its danger, as well as the certain ruin of interests of a superior order," *Regicide Peace* declared. "Often a man lost his all because he would not submit to hazard all in defending it." Burke demanded a reversal of "the whole line of that unprosperous prudence which hitherto had produced all the effects of the blindest temerity." This suggestive passage indicates that a false prudence eventuates in the same results as rashness.

While the French Revolution provoked Burke's strongest statements on the topic of boldness, it was not the only occasion for such reflections. In 1783 parliamentary debate on India, he said that "anything short" of bold reforms in the East India Company "would not only be delusive, but in this matter, which admits no medium, noxious in the extreme." Understanding which issues "admit[ted] no medium" was essential to prudence. In the *Reflections*, Burke recognized the necessity, in the face of the French danger, of overcoming his normal hesitation to address complex controversies: "If the prudence of reserve and decorum dictates silence in some circumstances, in others prudence of a higher order may justify us in speaking our thoughts." In his "Remarks on the Policy of the Allies with Respect to France," Burke warned that "if we meet this [Jacobin] energy with poor commonplace proceeding, with trivial maxims, paltry old saws, with doubts, fears, and suspicions, with a languid, uncertain hesitation, with a formal, official spirit, which is turned aside by every obstacle from its purpose, and which never sees a difficulty but to yield to it, or at best to evade it,—down we go to the bottom of the abyss, and nothing short of Omnipotence can save us." He added that because Britain had little to lose in France, and faced an entrenched power, "adventure, therefore, and not caution, is our policy. Here to be too presuming is the better error."

Burke's calls for boldness suggest several conclusions. One is that his standard remained the public safety, which in the case of Jacobinism he recognized was threatened by issues of a genuinely ultimate character. Recognizing these ultimate issues and distinguishing them from more mundane controversies was the task of prudence. Second, caution in these cases was inadvisable because it would not attain the desired end; it was, in this sense, the very essence of imprudence. The prudence that demands action over personal caution is a "prudence of a higher order."

Yet there is an intriguing qualification. Even in cases of "adventure" over "caution," Burke describes that course not as ideal but rather as "the better error." The formulation reflects another element of Burkean prudence: the capacity to choose not between good and bad but rather between greater and lesser evils.

Moderation and the Choice between Evils

Burke's *Thoughts on the Cause of the Present Discontents* was animated by a deep concern about the growing power of the court faction in England. Considering several remedies, he noted none was perfect: "It is no inconsiderable part of wisdom, to know how much of an evil ought to be tolerated; lest, by attempting a degree of purity impracticable in degenerate times and manners, instead of cutting off the subsisting ill-practices, new corruptions might be produced for the concealment and security of the old." This is an essential element of Burkean prudence. Purity was impossible both because times were "degenerate"—England was then in a period of political turmoil—but also because social life was complex. The pursuit of perfect rather than acceptable measures was not merely doomed, it was positively foolish: As Burke noted, it might simply lead to new corruptions, perhaps worse than the old. Much of politics involved this choice between evils. Both recognizing this fact and balancing the choices it entailed required prudence exactly because the issue could not be settled with philosophical precision. This was the case with taxation of the American colonies: "The spirit of practicability, of moderation, and mutual convenience will never call in geometrical exactness as the arbitrator of an amicable settlement."

Burke explained in *Discontents*: "It is a fallacy in constant use with those who would level all things, and confound right with wrong, to insist upon the inconveniences which are attached to every choice, without taking into consideration the different weight and consequence of those inconveniences. The question is not concerning *absolute* discontent or perfect satisfaction in government; neither of which can be pure and unmixed at any time, or upon any system." Explaining to the sheriffs of Bristol why he supported disclaiming Parliament's right to tax America, he wrote: "I parted with it as with a limb, but as a limb to save the body: and I would have parted with more, if more had been necessary; anything rather than a fruitless, hopeless, unnatural civil war." In the 1780 address to Parliament on shortening terms in the body, Burke averred: "It is wise to compass as many good ends as possibly you can, and, seeing there are inconveniences on both sides, with benefits on both, to give up a part of the benefit to soften the inconvenience."

Burke saw politics in terms of pursuing not the ideal but rather the least inconvenient measures available to fallen man. It was therefore necessary in the case of America to accommodate measures to reality. With respect to the "stubborn spirit" of the colonists, the choices were "to change that spirit, as inconvenient, by removing the causes,—to prosecute it as criminal,—or to comply with it, as necessary." The prudent course was accommodation to necessity, the rash option a fruitless and dangerous belief that something could, and ought to be, changed merely because it was "inconvenient." Defending his support for Irish trade to a Bristol constituent in 1778, Burke wrote that "it is a settled rule with me, to make the most of my *actual situation*; and not to refuse to do a proper thing, because there is something else more proper, which I am not able to do."

The path between evils was that of moderation—not, again, a geographic centrism that assumes virtue lies between shifting political antipodes, but rather a moral commitment to moderation as a prudent accommodation to the limits of human wisdom. Conciliation with the colonies was consequently not only the moderate but also the realistic choice, he told the sheriffs of Bristol: "I know many have been taught to think that moderation in a case like this is a sort of treason,—and that all arguments for it are sufficiently answered by railing at rebels and rebellion....But I would wish them, in this grave matter, and if peace is not wholly removed from their hearts, to consider seriously...that to criminate and recriminate never yet was the road to reconciliation, in any difference amongst men."

This was why Burke, writing to the sheriffs of Bristol, described prudence as "the god of this lower world," with the emphasis on "lower." Human conditions were unsuited to divine perfection. "And yet I have lived to see prudence and conformity to circumstances wholly set at nought [*sic*] in our late controversies, and treated as if they were the most contemptible and irrational of all things." Seeking perfection was outright dangerous because government always entailed inconvenience, which was why prudence was necessary to achieve a balance. In 1780, he opposed shortening parliamentary terms for this reason:

> That man thinks much too highly, and therefore he thinks weakly and delusively, of any contrivance of human wisdom, who believes that it can make any sort of approach to perfection. There is not, there never was, a principle of government under heaven, that does not, in the very pursuit of the good it proposes, naturally and inevitably lead into some inconvenience which makes it absolutely necessary to counterwork and weaken the application of that first principle itself, and to abandon something of the extent of the advantage you proposed by it, in order to prevent also the inconveniences which have arisen from the instrument of all the good you had in view.

The reason Burke feared "moderation [being] stigmatized as the virtue of cowards, and compromise as the prudence of traitors" was precisely that it would force even politicians disposed to moderation to act in extremes to preserve their credibility for more accommodating circumstances. For like reasons, the *Reflections* supported the balancing mechanisms of the British constitution because "they interpose a salutary check to all precipitate resolutions. They render deliberation a matter, not of choice, but of necessity; they make all change a subject of compromise, which naturally begets moderation...."

Early in the French Revolution, Burke remarked to the Earl of Charlemont that "[m]en must have a certain fund of natural moderation to qualify them for Freedom, else it become noxious to themselves and a perfect Nuisance to everybody else." In a prescient November 1789 letter to his French correspondent Charles-Jean-François Depont, an epistle he would later expand into the *Reflections*, Burke explained: "[I]n all changes in the State, Moderation is a Virtue not only Amiable but powerful. It is a disposing, arranging, conciliating, cementing Virtue. In the formation of New Constitutions it is in its Province...."

These considerations led Burke to two of his most important rules of prudence: never to reason for the ordinary case from the extreme case and never to carry principles to their logical extremes. One reason Parliament could be less fearful of the American colonists was that their ordinary conduct should not be judged while they were inflamed. "It is, besides, a very great mistake to imagine that mankind follow up practically any speculative principle, either of government or of freedom, as far as it will go in argument and logical illation." In the *Appeal from the New to the Old Whigs*, he explained that "the whole scheme of our mixed Constitution is to prevent any one of its principles from being carried as far as, taken by itself, and theoretically, it would go." The reason not to take principles to their extreme was that doing so divorced them from both circumstances and modesty. As Harvey C. Mansfield, one of Burke's closest readers, put it, "In the course of generalization, limited actions undertaken with great circumspection and compunction in the extreme case are transformed into wanton, irresponsible destructiveness in the universal case."

Burke thus explained in the *Reflections* that the Glorious Revolution of 1688 did not license future rebellions: It aimed, instead, to be "a parent of settlement, and not a nursery of future revolutions." The events of 1688 constituted an exception, not a rule, and "it is against all genuine principles of jurisprudence to draw a principle from a law made in a special case and regarding an individual person." Nor was there any inconsistency involved in this position. "It is far from impossible to reconcile, if we do not suffer ourselves to be entangled in the mazes of metaphysic sophistry, the use both of a fixed rule and an occasional deviation...." Similarly, Burke opposed speculation for speculation's sake. As early as 1780, he wrote to his Bristol friend Joseph Harford that the endemic weakness of the Whig Party had been "the admission among them of the Corps of Schemers; who in reality, and at bottom, mean little more than to indulge themselves with Speculations; but who do us infinite Mischief, by persuading many sober and well meaning people, that we have designs inconsistent with the Constitution left to us by our forefathers. You know how many are startled with the Idea of innovation." On Burke's account, people were not wrong to be startled by innovation when it was undertaken for its own sake, for it tended to be disconnected from limiting principles.

Burke likewise argued in the *Appeal* that "[o]ur courts cannot be more fearful in suffering fictitious cases to be brought before them for eliciting their determination on a point of law than prudent moralists are in putting extreme and hazardous cases of conscience upon emergencies not existing." Even "the very habit of stating these extreme cases is not very laudable or safe; because, in general, it is not right to turn our

duties into doubts." The natural effect of reasoning from extremes was
to corrode principles and customs in the ordinary case. Moreover, the
extremes rarely stayed confined to the theoretical realm. Only the "moral
sentiments" of the few could secure society against those pursuing "the
utmost extremities," "wild conceits," and "savage theories," the *Appeal*
continued. These theories were dangerous precisely because the French
could not restrain themselves from putting them into effect, in which
case reason intoxicated with confidence in itself recognized no principle
of limitation. Burke warned Lord Grenville, the British foreign secretary,
of this in 1792, cataloging the abuses of the Revolution and noting they
were done "at a time when theories are rashly formed and readily pass
from speculation into practice...."

In 1792, Burke responded in Parliament to a petition in which the
Unitarian Society sought a relaxation of religious regulations. Suspecting
the Society of Jacobin sympathies, he said he supported religious liberty
but, with the French Revolution assuming an imperial and expansionist
countenance, the issue had to be judged according to circumstances rather
than abstractions: "Crude, unconnected truths are in the world of practice what falsehoods are in theory. A reasonable, prudent, provident, and
moderate coercion may be a means of preventing acts of extreme ferocity
and rigor: for by propagating excessive and extravagant doctrines, such
extravagant disorders take place as require the most perilous and fierce
corrections to oppose them." The "crude" and "unconnected" nature of
these "truths" was what made them imprudent.

There was another reason for intellectual restraint: The scope of human reason was limited, especially when applied to the infinite complexity
of political life. Burke warned in the *Appeal* against the capacity of reason
to comprehend the whole of human society:

> An ignorant man, who is not fool enough to meddle with his clock, is,
> however, sufficiently confident to think he can safely take to pieces and
> put together, at his pleasure, a moral machine of another guise, impor-
> tance, and complexity, composed of far other wheels and springs and
> balances and counteracting and cooperating powers. Men little think how
> immorally they act in rashly meddling with what they do not understand.
> Their delusive good intention is no sort of excuse for their presumption.
> They who truly mean well must be fearful of acting ill.

It is striking that rashness is not merely misguided but patently "immoral" because it spurns humility. This spirit is one of "presumption," as opposed to the prudent ethic that is "fearful" of erring in the attempted destruction and recomposition of society. In 1793, Burke wrote to the Irish statesman Sir Lawrence Parsons that it was "unfortunate that after having enjoyd [*sic*] for so many ages the Benefits of civil Society...one should be obliged at every turn to recur to the analysis of that society to convince men by abstract reasoning of the value of the benefits which they ought to know by feeling, and to enjoy with gratitude. The Evil of our time is in presumption and malice, the latter partly the Cause, partly the consequence of the former." The presumptuous man was not merely misguided, but malicious.

Because presumption, which he told the sheriffs of Bristol was "not becoming a Christian man," results from a narrowed view, prudence requires an enlargement of perspective. Lawyers, he said in the speech on American taxation, are trained in "one of the first and noblest of human sciences," but this schooling is narrow and is consequently "not apt, except in persons very happily born, to open and to liberalize the mind exactly in the same proportion." He expanded on this theme to the sheriffs of Bristol: While lawyers had to obey strict rules, "legislators ought to do what lawyers cannot; for they have no other rules to bind them but the great principles of reason and equity and the general sense of mankind" and should "enlarge and enlighten the law" rather than "bind their higher capacity" by overly strict constructions. The prudence this required distinguished political judgment from legal precision.

Similarly, the *Reflections* argued, no "great prudence" was required simply to establish a government. But a free government must be the work of "a sagacious, powerful, and combining mind." The word that intrigues is "combining": Prudence entailed putting the complex elements of history and contemporary society together. The *Reflections* similarly called political reason—that is, prudence—a "computing principle: adding, subtracting, multiplying, and dividing, morally, and not metaphysically, or mathematically, true moral denominations." Prudence, *Regicide Peace* explained, is "a cool, steady, deliberate principle...informed, moderated, and directed by an enlarged knowledge of its great public ends...."

These are suggestive formulations. The prudent statesman must be able to combine different strands of knowledge and, more importantly, "the conjunctions and oppositions of men and things," that is, principle and circumstance. This prudence is by its very nature inexact; as we shall see in treating Burke's view of reason in Chapter 3, the quest for mathematical precision in politics and morals was both foolhardy and dangerous. Burke also suggested that while constitutions should be complex—"when I hear the simplicity of contrivance aimed at and boasted of in any new political constitutions, I am at no loss to decide that the artificers are grossly ignorant of their trade or totally negligent of their duty," he wrote of the Revolutionary French Constitution in the *Reflections*—policies should not be. His speech on conciliation with the American colonies declared:

> The proposition is peace. Not peace through the medium of war; not peace to be hunted through the labyrinth of intricate and endless negotiations; not peace to arise out of universal discord, fomented from principle, in all parts of the empire; not peace to depend on the juridical determination of perplexing questions, or the precise marking the shadowy boundaries of a complex government. It is simple peace, sought in its natural course and in its ordinary haunts....Refined policy ever has been the parent of confusion....

The choice between evils also reflected Burke's emphasis on a core conservative principle: limitation. In the letter to Depont, Burke explained that limits were necessary even, perhaps especially, with respect to good things: "[E]very day's account shows more and more, in my opinion, the ill-consequence of keeping good principles, and good general views, within no bounds." In a 1793 parliamentary speech, he declared that France "was an enemy to limited monarchy, as monarchy, and to the limitation, as limitation." The importance of limitation was that it, too, reflected a modesty about human reason's capacity to grasp the intricacies of society and an emphasis on moderation. Limitation conserves; innovation revolts.

Revolution and Reform

Yuval Levin notes that "Burke's opposition to the French Revolution, especially as laid out in the *Reflections*, involves a contrast between two modes of political change, rather than between two types of regime or views of politics. The contrast Burke draws in the *Reflections* between France and Britain is really a contrast between revolution and reform." Revolution was inherently hostile to limitation. Burke argued in the *Reflections* that if "a prudent man were obliged to make a choice of what errors and excesses of enthusiasm he would condemn or bear, perhaps he would think the superstition which builds to be more tolerable than that which demolishes,—that which adorns a country, than that which deforms it,—that which endows, than that which plunders,—that which disposes to mistaken beneficence, than that which stimulates to real injustice...." Perhaps no aspect of prudence requires a greater dose of that virtue than assessing the need for, and knowing the difference between, revolution and reform.

Burke was accused of inconsistency for supporting the American colonists, the rights of Irish Catholics, and the people of India, yet opposing the French Revolution. The difference, though, was between reform and revolution, the former of which sought to adjust policies to restore ancient principles, the latter to capsize them. He wrote of France in the *Reflections* that "anything which unnecessarily tore to pieces the contexture of the state not only prevented all real reformation, but introduced evils which would call, but perhaps call in vain, for new reformation." In any case, "a revolution will be the last resource of the thinking and the good," regardless of whether it had right on its side. Man had natural rights, but society was artificial, and shredding it meant not only discarding an inheritance but also returning to a savage and primitive state. Revolutionaries were fanatics nearly by definition and brutal as a result of their fanaticism. The French Revolution could not even claim the scant redemption of committing cruelties from "the base result of fear." It did so from ideology ("a Revolution of doctrine and theoretic dogma," in the formulation of *Thoughts on French Affairs*), which was more dangerous: "The worst of these politics of revolution is this: they temper and harden the breast, in order to prepare it for the desperate strokes which are sometimes used in extreme occasions."

It is important that revolution *precluded* reform by destroying institutions that would have enabled it. He thus wrote to Depont that without a sound constitution that limited liberty, "[y]ou may have made a Revolution, but not a Reformation." Burke himself was a lifelong

reformer whose opposition to Jacobin radicalism was entirely consistent. Early in the *Reflections*, he declared his belief that "a state without
the means of some change is without the means of its conservation."
It is "conservation" that opens a window into Burke's thought on the
topic. Immediately before the passage we have already encountered on
"moral" rather than "complexional" timidity, Burke delineated criteria
for reform: "I would not exclude alteration neither; but even when I
changed, it should be to preserve. I should be led to my remedy by a
great grievance. In what I did, I should follow the example of our ancestors. I would make the reparation as nearly as possible in the style
of the building." The purpose of reformation, in other words, was the
restoration of customary principles that, as we shall see, Burke viewed
as the storehouse of generational wisdom.

Conserving reform requires prudence calibrated to the extent of the
danger it seeks to remedy. In Parliament in 1783, Burke supported total reform of the East India Company because the corporation was "absolutely
incorrigible." The American colonists were reformers, not revolutionaries,
a difference to which Burke alluded in explaining in the *Appeal* that if
"the Americans had rebelled merely in order to enlarge their liberty, [he]
would have thought very differently of the American cause." Instead,
they rebelled to restore their prior relation to the mother country, a far
more modest project.

Nonetheless, even reform should be sparing because overuse makes it
unavailable when it is truly necessary. He wrote in the *Reflections*: "This
distemper of remedy, grown habitual, relaxes and wears out, by a vulgar
and prostituted use, the spring of that spirit which is to be exerted on
great occasions." The "extreme medicine of the Constitution [should not
be] its daily bread. It renders the habit of society dangerously valetudi-
nary; it is taking periodical doses of mercury sublimate, and swallowing
down repeated provocative of cantharides to our love of liberty." Prudent
reform both reconciles the public to change and helps statesmen undertake that change gradually and therefore safely. "By a slow, but well-sus-
tained progress, the effect of each step is watched; the good or ill success
of the first gives light to us in the second; and so, from light to light, we
are conducted with safety through the whole series."

Reform also required prudence in another sense: the capacity and
willingness to deal with difficult problems. The French were unwilling

to do so, so they engaged in a rampage of indiscriminate destruction of political and social institutions. This, Burke wrote in the *Reflections*, was unimpressive: If the tactic was wanton destruction, a mob would do just as well as legislators: "Rage and frenzy will pull down more in half an hour than prudence, deliberation, and foresight can build up in a hundred years." Reform was a far more challenging undertaking, and natural critics, especially puritanical perfectionists, were unsuited to it. "[T]hose who are habitually employed in finding and displaying faults are unqualified for the work of reformation; because their minds are not only unfurnished with patterns of the fair and good, but by habit they come to take no delight in the contemplation of those things. By hating vices too much, they come to love men too little."

As an exception to a nearly universal rule, revolution "is a measure which, *prima fronte*, requires an apology." Burke meant apology in the sense of justification, and he specified that "common reasons" could not "justify so violent a proceeding." Men should be sparing "in the voluntary production of evil," the *Appeal* argued. "Every revolution contains in it something of evil." Most revolutions are motivated by power and result in rapacity, whereas, according to *Regicide Peace*, "[t]he blood of man should never be shed but to redeem the blood of man. It is well shed for our family, for our friends, for our God, for our country, for our kind. The rest is vanity; the rest is crime." This accusation of vanity accentuates the extent to which, in Burke's view, revolutionaries were typically bent on seeing themselves as saviors and acquiring the power that comes with that status.

No one was so vain as innovators. Burke's *Letter to a Noble Lord*, written to defend the modest privileges he had received from the crown, reminded his correspondent: "It cannot at this time be too often repeated, line upon line, precept upon precept, until it comes into the currency of a proverb,—To innovate is not to reform. The French revolutionists complained of everything; they refused to reform anything; and they left nothing, no, nothing at all, *unchanged*." This is Burke's innate conservatism. Conserving reform is the epitome of prudence and the opposite of innovation. Burke championed economic reforms that reduced the power of the court faction, but later explained them in the *Letter to a Noble Lord* this way: "It was, then, not my love, but my hatred to innovation, that produced my plan of reform."

Prudence and the "Ultimate Object"

We have seen that Burke associated prudence with "moral caution" but
also with "stead[iness]" and conviction. Each was necessary to identify the
correct path toward right ends. He wrote to the Duke of Portland in 1780
that prudence must be oriented toward ends rather than becoming an
end in itself: "I hope I never shall reject the principles of general publick
prudence; Those which go under the description of the moral Virtue of
that name; but as to the prudence of giving up the principle to the means,
I confess I grow ten times more restive than ever."

Prudence entailed an "enlarged" mind capable of "combining" infor-
mation," a capacity learned from the variegated experience of history. The
prudent statesman was forever choosing between evils, a path that helped
encourage moderation. All this was morally grounded. "If circumspection
and caution are a part of wisdom, when we work only upon inanimate
matter," Burke wrote in the *Reflections*, "surely they become a part of
duty too, when the subject of our demotion and construction is not brick
and timber, but sentient beings, by the sudden alteration of whose state,
condition, and habits, multitudes may be rendered miserable." This is not
to say, again, that Burke advocated timidity. The *Reflections* advocated
steadiness: "The true lawgiver ought to have a heart full of sensibility. He
ought to love and respect his kind, and to fear himself. It may be allowed
to his temperament to catch his ultimate object with an intuitive glance;
but his movements towards it ought to be deliberate."

Such were Lincoln's movements, and his conception of prudence, to
which we now turn.

CHAPTER TWO

✌ ✾

The Family of the Lion, or the Tribe of the Eagle

Lincoln on Prudence

In 1836, seeking reelection to the Illinois legislature, a 27-year-old Lincoln delivered his sparse platform to the editor of his hometown *Sangamo Journal* in New Salem, Illinois. The only specific issues he mentioned were expanding suffrage and the Whig staple of internal improvements: the use of federal funds for canals, railroads, and the like. Instead of a laundry list of specific issues, Lincoln offered a principle of representation: "If elected, I shall consider the whole people of Sangamon my constituents, as well those that oppose, as those that support me. While acting as their representative, I shall be governed by their will, on all subjects upon which I have the means of knowing what their will is; and upon all others, I shall do what my own judgment teaches me will best advance their interests." This chapter examines the elements of Lincoln's judgment: how he formed it, and how he exercised it.

In Lincoln's case, like Burke's, prudence demanded accommodation but not surrender to circumstances. Lincoln is in many ways both a more elusive and a more complex figure than Burke on this score. He is more elusive because we must extract the dimensions of his prudence from his public acts and statements, which were offered not in book-length tracts or even parliamentary stemwinders, but rather in comparatively brief addresses, correspondence, and state papers, typically less philosophical than political. Lincoln is more complex because those circumstances, most obviously serving in an executive capacity during a time of rebellion, more often called for bold strokes that, if we do not attend to them carefully, mask the character of his prudence. In Burke's case, it is necessary to accentuate the importance of boldness in the thought of a statesman whose prudence was so inflected with caution. In Lincoln's, we must reverse this sequence, beginning with the guarded and gradualist nature of his politics so we can see them emerge in his decisive presidential leadership.

Prudence and Caution

In the epigraph to this study, we saw Lincoln, writing to the newly appointed commander of the Army of the Potomac, General Joseph Hooker, in January 1863, commend "energy" and "vigilance" as distinctly opposed to "rashness." Lincoln had been through a series of commanders whose inactivity and excessive caution vexed him. He was not trying to have it both ways. His statesmanship was always energetic in the sense we saw Burke counsel at the close of Chapter 1: steady, stubborn progress toward long-term goals. Yet Lincoln also opposed rash, impassioned politics. The weight and chastening restraint of his rhetoric seemed to grow with the gravity of the crisis he faced.

Lincoln's executive leadership and his entry into the highest realm of the American pantheon have caused one of his earliest reflections on this topic, the Lyceum Address of 1838—delivered to a club of young men in Springfield, Illinois, and addressing the dangers of the political ambition for greatness—often to be read in retrospective irony. Yet the address is of a piece with his later writings and actions. The difference is that circumstances changed. The calibration of action to circumstance was the core of Lincoln's prudence. In 1838, the nation prosperous and secure, it seemed to Lincoln that the greatest danger to liberty would be the pursuit of greatness in times that did not require it.

Lincoln opened the speech by grounding republicanism in "the *attachment* of the People," which he warned would be undermined by the spread of mob law across the land. Vigilantism was practiced by both "the pleasure hunting masters of Southern slaves, and"—in a suggestive formulation—"the order loving citizens of the land of steady habits," by which he apparently meant the Western states. In a manner typical of his prudent rhetoric, Lincoln put the issue of the lynching of abolitionists and African Americans in terms to which his broad audience could relate: In addition to its inherent injustice and the proclivity of mobs to err in their judgments of innocence and guilt, vigilante justice threatened "the perpetuation of our political institutions." These, he said, noting the geographical security of the country, could only be eroded from within, not attacked from abroad. If the people came to believe their government could not protect them, their loyalty to it would diminish, paving the way for demagogic tyrants: "men of sufficient talent and ambition [who] will not be wanting to seize the opportunity, strike the blow, and overturn that fair fabric, which for the last half century, has been the fondest hope, of the lovers of freedom, throughout the world."

Lincoln's solution to this at first glance seems immoderate: "Let every American, every lover of liberty, every well wisher to his posterity, swear by the blood of the Revolution, never to violate in the least particular, the laws of the country; and never to tolerate their violation by others." But this seeming inflexibility regardless of circumstances, even immoderation ("in the least particular")—which Lincoln describes as a "political religion"—turns out to have a more pliable side. Bad laws exist and "should be repealed as soon as possible," but obeyed while in force unless—and this is a considerable exception—they are "too intolerable."

More important, why was this zeal in the observance of the law required? The reason was another danger to liberty that illustrates the decisive importance of caution in Lincoln's prudence: excess ambition. The superficial irony of this fear is unmistakable. As Allen C. Guelzo, among others, has noted, Lincoln was an ambitious man profoundly concerned about leaving a mark on the world. That makes it all the more striking that the Lyceum Address seems to be an exercise in chastening and channeling his own ambition.

During the American Revolution, Lincoln explained, circumstances naturally channeled ambition toward admirable ends: "Then, all that sought celebrity and fame, and distinction, expected to find them in the success of that experiment. Their all was staked upon it:—their destiny was inseparably linked with it. Their ambition aspired to display before an admiring world, a practical demonstration of the truth of a proposition, which had hitherto been considered, at best no better, than problematical; namely, the capability of a people to govern themselves." But now the period of founding a new regime had passed and—here we arrive at the prudence of the Lyceum Address—it now would become challenging to pursue rightful ends by moderate means. "[T]he game is caught; and I believe it is true, that with the catching, end the pleasures of the chase. This field of glory is harvested, and the crop is already appropriated. But new reapers will arise, and they, too, will seek a field." Those who thrive on glory would not be able to find it in maintaining a regime established by others, but they would find it nonetheless.

These members of "the family of the lion, or the tribe of the eagle," would never be satisfied with merely occupying office and governing prudently in quiet times:

> What! think you these places would satisfy an Alexander, a Caesar, or a Napoleon? Never! Towering genius disdains a beaten path. It seeks regions hitherto unexplored. It sees no distinction in adding story to story, upon the monuments of fame, erected to the memory of others. It denies that it is glory enough to serve under any chief. It scorns to tread in the footsteps of any predecessor, however illustrious. It thirsts and burns for distinction; and, if possible, it will have it, whether at the expense of emancipating slaves, or enslaving freemen.

Moreover, the "interesting scenes of the revolution" had the effect of constructively absorbing "the *passions* of the people as distinguished from their judgment. By this influence, the jealousy, envy, and avarice, incident to our nature, and so common to a state of peace, prosperity, and conscious strength, were, for the time, in a great measure smothered and rendered inactive; while the deep rooted principles of hate, and the powerful motive of revenge, instead of being turned against each other, were directed exclusively against the British nation." This antinomy between "passions" and "judgment," which we shall explore in treating Lincoln's idea of reason in Chapter 4, is key to his prudence. The memories of the Revolution "*were* the pillars of the temple of liberty" but in peaceful times, passion would become an enemy rather than an ally. "Reason, cold, calculating, unimpassioned reason, must furnish all the materials for our future support and defence."

As Weaver has noted, and as Chapters 3 and 4 will observe, this differs unmistakably from Burke's emphasis on human sympathy and circumstantial reasoning. Lincoln was a more axiomatic thinker than Burke, who tended to emphasize feeling over cold logic. Still, the Lyceum Address was a model of Lincolnian prudence. He sought to calibrate actions to circumstances, such that calm times, like those he wrongly foresaw continuing, elicited calm leadership. Boldness, as this chapter will later show, was warranted in times of crisis. The conflation of calm and crisis threatened liberty by deranging prudence because actions did not comport with conditions on the ground. In this sense, the differences between Burke and Lincoln should be observed but not overstated. Circumstances, for Lincoln as for Burke, grounded such qualities as reason, which might otherwise burst their proper limits. It is therefore significant that the form of reason we needed was "sober," a sharp contrast with the philosophical fanaticism that Burke detested in the French Revolution.

Lincoln's address to Springfield's Washington Temperance Society, a group named after the country's father and devoted to eradicating alcohol abuse, similarly counseled moderation, not simply in drink but also in the tones in which it was discouraged. When alcoholics and liquor merchants were addressed not "by erring man to an erring brother; but in the thundering tones of anathema and denunciation," they could not hear the message. Lincoln characterized these "old school champions" of temperance as seeking a "wise" goal but forsaking "judicious" means—the essence of imprudence.

Lincoln accommodated moralism to human reality. He recognized, for example, the difficulty of instilling temperance by appealing to distant benefits or future generations. "What an ignorance of human nature does it exhibit, to ask or expect a whole community to rise up and labor for the *temporal* happiness of *others* after *themselves* shall be consigned to the dust, a majority of which community take no pains whatever to secure their own eternal welfare, at a no greater distant day?" His rejection of moralism was further evident in Lincoln's humble refusal to boast of his own temperance. "In my judgment, such of us as have never fallen victims, have been spared more from the absence of appetite, than from any mental or moral superiority over those who have." On the contrary, "drunkards as a class" tended to have better heads and hearts.

Lincoln's emphasis on steadiness and sober prudence was also clear in two eulogies he gave in the early 1850s, one for President Zachary Taylor and the other for the Whig statesman Henry Clay. Lincoln extolled Taylor's military record: "Gen. Taylor's battles were not distinguished for brilliant military manouevers; but in all, he seems rather to have conquered by the exercise of a sober and steady judgment, coupled with a dogged incapacity to understand that defeat was possible. His rarest military trait, was a combination of negatives—absence of *excitement* and absence of *fear*."

This combination is exactly what he later commended to General Hooker, and it was the essence of prudence. Clay, "my beau ideal of a statesman," Lincoln once said, exemplified similar qualities. Eulogizing Clay, Lincoln observed that the Kentuckian "owed his pre-eminence to no one quality, but to a fortunate combination of several." Among these were the essential ingredients of prudence. "His judgment was excellent.... His will was indomitable...." Indomitable will, significantly, was entirely compatible with the prudence Clay exhibited on the slavery controversy, on which "his feeling and his judgment...ever led him to oppose both extremes of opinion on the subject."

Moderate Means and Ultimate Goals

The slavery controversy was the clearest example of Lincoln's prudence, which took the form not of accommodating himself to evil but rather of alleviating it gradually. He wrote to his friend Williamson Durley in 1845 that abolitionist inflexibility on the subject had cost Clay the presidency in 1844, when the pro-slavery James K. Polk was elected because Whigs were split. "If the whig abolitionists of New York had voted with us last fall, Mr. Clay would now be president, whig principles in the ascendent, and [the slave state] Texas not annexed; whereas by the division, all that either had at stake in the contest, was lost." Like Burke, Lincoln understood the need to choose between unsatisfactory options in political life. The abolitionists who withheld their votes from Clay did not understand this, preferring instead, as one told Lincoln: "We are not to do evil that good may come." Lincoln, writing to Durley, replied: "This general, proposition is doubtless correct; but did it apply? If by your votes you could have prevented the *extention*, &c. of slavery, would it not have been *good* and not *evil* so to have used your votes, even though it involved the casting of them for a slaveholder?"

Yet Lincoln, still writing to Durley, nonetheless fixed his long-range vision on the end of slavery. "I hold it to be a paramount duty of us in the free states, due to the Union of the states, and perhaps to liberty itself (paradox though it may seem) to let the slavery of the other states alone; while, on the other hand, I hold it to be equally clear, that we should never knowingly lend ourselves directly or indirectly, to prevent that slavery from dying a natural death...."This was not paradoxical; it was a prudent accommodation to the complexities of political life.

In the Peoria Address of 1854—delivered in response to the Kansas-Nebraska Act's decision to repeal the Missouri Compromise, which forbade slavery in the territories, in favor of allowing the two new states to vote on the institution—Lincoln was unmistakable in articulating his principles. "Slavery is founded in the selfishness of man's nature—opposition to it, is his love of justice." Yet this very antagonism was so sharp that compromise was necessary. Slavery, however, should be permitted in then-slaveholding states only out of "necessity," the same reason, he said at Peoria, that the constitutional framers accommodated themselves to it. Necessity, it is important to note, was a limiting rather than a licensing principle: "Let us turn slavery from its claims of 'moral right,' back upon its existing legal rights, and its arguments of 'necessity.'"

Lincoln was reacting to the rising argument in the South that slavery was not a necessary evil but rather a positive good, and as Diana Schaub has noted, his purpose was to enlarge public opinion even as he accommodated himself to it. Lincoln said in the first Lincoln-Douglas debate that "he who moulds public sentiment, goes deeper than he who enacts statutes or pronounces decisions. He makes statutes and decisions possible or impossible to be executed." This accommodation was another element of Lincoln's prudence, for he realized that the supremacy of public opinion in a republic required statesmen to move gradually. He told a Republican banquet in Chicago in 1856: "Our government rests in public opinion. Whoever can change public opinion, can change the government, practically just so much."

Lincoln sought to anchor public opinion in the Declaration's promise of equality. Since 1776, history had been "a steady progress" toward that ideal. But steadiness was key. Lincoln often spoke of slavery's "ultimate

extinction," which he described in a later Chicago speech as the position
of an "Old Line Whig." He noted in a fragment he wrote on slavery
in 1858 that abolition in Great Britain took a century. In Chicago in
1858, he assessed the Biblical imperative, "As your Father in Heaven is
perfect, be ye also perfect." Moral perfection, Lincoln explained, could
be attained only in degrees. "So I say in relation to the principle that all
men are created equal, let it be as nearly reached as we can. If we cannot
give freedom to every creature, let us do nothing that will impose slavery
upon any other creature."

There was another sense in which slavery forced a Burkean choice
between evils. Abolition, Lincoln knew, would rend the Union, so the
question was not between slavery and abolition but rather between abolition and union. "[H]ow much," Lincoln wrote to his old friend Joshua
Speed in 1855, "the great body of the Northern people do crucify their
feelings, in order to maintain their loyalty to the constitution and the
Union." This had been the conundrum at the framing of the Constitution,
he told a Springfield audience in 1858: "The framers of the Constitution
found the institution of slavery amongst their other institutions at the
time. They found that by an effort to eradicate it, they might lose much of
what they had already gained. They were obliged to bow to the necessity."

Even when he spoke of a prudent approach to the issue, Lincoln
sought to establish the rights of African Americans. In the 1858 Springfield speech, Lincoln denied that the Declaration meant "that all men
were created equal in all respects," but his purpose in saying so was to
pivot to the sense in which equality did obtain: "Certainly the negro is
not our equal in color—perhaps not in many other respects; still, in the
right to put into his mouth the bread that his own hands have earned, he
is the equal of every other man, white or black." The immediate imperative
provoked by the Kansas-Nebraska issue was to stop the spread of slavery
into unorganized territories. These territories were explicitly different,
Lincoln often said, from ones in which slavery was long entrenched.
Clay, for example, had said that he would oppose slavery in a state of
nature. Lincoln wrote to J. U. Brown in 1858: "Exactly so. In our new free
territories, a state of nature does exist. In them Congress lays the foundations of society; and, in laying those foundations, I say, with Mr. Clay,
it is desirable that the declaration of the equality of all men shall be kept
in view, as a great fundamental principle; and that Congress, which lays

the foundations of society, should, like Mr. Clay, be strongly opposed to the incorporation of slavery among its elements."

Gradualism, Accommodation, and Accession

Because of the unavoidable circumstance that slavery existed in the South, Lincoln preferred gradual emancipation as a means of slowly habituating slaveholders to the institution's end. In the sixth Lincoln-Douglas debate, Lincoln sounded the essence of prudence: "Because we think [slavery] wrong, we propose a course of policy that shall deal with it as a wrong. We deal with it as with any other wrong, in so far as we can prevent its growing any larger, and so deal with it that in the run of time there may be some promise of an end to it." Any Republican who did not believe slavery was evil should leave the party. "[O]n the other hand, if there be any man in the Republican party who is impatient over the necessity springing from its actual presence, and is impatient of the constitutional guarantees thrown around it, and would act in disregard of these, he too is misplaced standing with us. He will find his place somewhere else; for we have a due regard, so far as we are capable of understanding them, for all these things." The regard he had for circumstances was not complete, only the amount that was "due," producing a combination of firm principle and appropriate means: prudence defined.

Speaking in Chicago in 1859, Lincoln acknowledged both ultimate principle and the prudence necessary to attain it: "The Republican principle, the profound central truth that slavery is wrong and ought to be dealt with as a wrong, though we are always to remember the fact of its actual existence amongst us and faithfully observe all the constitutional guarantees—the unalterable principle never for a moment to be lost sight of that it is a wrong and ought to be dealt with as such." But the best way to deal with it might entail a gradual approach. "I suppose [slavery] may long exist, and perhaps the best way for it to come to an end peaceably is for it to exist for a length of time. But I say that the spread and strengthening and perpetuation of it is an entirely different proposition."

In 1859, this prudence led Lincoln to caution Representative Schuyler Colfax of Indiana, the future Speaker of the House and a founder of the Republican Party, to join him in ensuring that especially explosive issues were excluded from a national Republican convention. Regional inflexibility

on regional issues, such as anti-immigrant sentiment or opposition to the
Fugitive Slave Act, would "explode" a convention and distract its members
from their larger object: the eventual end of slavery. "I write this for your
eye only," he told Colfax, "hoping however that if you see danger as I
think I do, you will do what you can to avert it." Speaking in Cincinnati
later that year, Lincoln maintained this national perspective. Slavery was
immovably wrong, he explained, and must be treated as such. "When I
say this, I do not mean to say that this general government is charged
with the duty of redressing or preventing all the wrongs in the world; but
I do think that it is charged with the duty of preventing and redressing
all wrongs which are wrongs to itself." The national government was
"expressly charged with the duty of providing for the general welfare,"
which the expansion of slavery violated. The standard was the common
good, which was why Lincoln would not endorse "interfer[ing] with the
institution of slavery in the states where it exists, because the constitution
forbids it, and the general welfare does not require us to do so."

The law of the Constitution was binding, but the statesman had to
exercise prudence within its boundaries. In the Cooper Union Address
of February 1860, Lincoln explained: "No one who has sworn to support
the Constitution, can conscientiously vote for what he understands to be
an unconstitutional measure, however expedient he may think it; but one
may and ought to vote against a measure which he deems constitutional,
if, at the same time, he deems it inexpedient." Still, Republicans must
recognize the ultimate value of union and the necessity of its maintenance to slavery's ultimate end. *Even though much provoked, let us do
nothing through passion and ill temper. Even though the southern people will
not so much as listen to us, let us calmly consider their demands, and yield to
them if, in our deliberate view of our duty, we possibly can.* This prudence
precluded Lincoln from employing against slavery "the thundering tones
of anathema and denunciation" he had repudiated in the Temperance
Address. In the Peoria Address, he had likewise allowed: "[I] think I
have no prejudice against the Southern people. They are just what we
would be in their situation. If slavery did not now exist amongst them,
they would not introduce it. If it did now exist amongst us, we should
not instantly give it up."

In the period between his 1860 election and his 1861 inauguration,
Lincoln prudently refrained from remarks that would bind him in office

even as the dissolution of the Union commenced. But his First Inaugural was a model of prudent conciliation oriented to ultimate principle. He disclaimed any intention to "construe the Constitution or laws, by any hypercritical rules," by which he meant he would not hunt for technicalities on which to base limitations on slavery. He denied a need for "bloodshed or violence." Lincoln continued, confining himself to the realities on the ground: "[I]n every case and exigency, my best direction will be exercised, according to circumstances actually existing," the same standard he had declared in his letter to the *Sangamo Journal* while running for the Illinois statehouse a quarter-century before. Harnessing the realities of circumstance as a principle of limitation suggests Burkean prudence, as in Lincoln's observation of the literal impossibility of separation between adjacent states: "Physically speaking, we cannot separate. We cannot remove our respective sections from each other, nor build an impassable wall between them."

Lincoln urged a similar ethic of prudent judgment on the South: "Will you hazard so desperate a step [as secession], while there is any possibility that any portion of the ills you fly from, have no real existence? Will you, while the certain ills you fly to, are greater than all the real ones you fly from? Will you risk the commission of so fearful a mistake?" This is caution grounded in calculation, and it evokes Burke's standard for choosing between evils: Known harms should be emphasized over hypothetical risks. As the First Inaugural built toward its rhetorical denouement—it had theretofore sounded more like a legal brief, a deliberate exercise in rhetorical restraint—Lincoln urged "a patient confidence in the ultimate justice of the people." This was the reconciliation of principle and prudence: Justice was to be attained (principle) but the path to it would unfold ultimately over time (prudence). He sought prudence on all sides: "My countrymen, one and all, think calmly and well, upon this whole subject. Nothing valuable can be lost by taking time. If there be an object to *hurry* any of you, in hot haste, to a step which you would never take *deliberately*, that object will be frustrated by taking time; but no good object can be frustrated by it."

As president, Lincoln's accommodation to circumstance led him to order commanding General Winfield Scott to allow the Maryland legislature to assemble in 1861 despite the risk that it would vote to secede. This was not acceding to circumstance; as his order to Scott indicates, accommodating to it is different from accession because accommodation pursues rather than surrenders ultimate goals. Lincoln told Scott that preventing a meeting of the legislature "would not be justifiable; nor, efficient for the desired object." That is, arresting or dispersing members of the legislature would be imprudent because it would not permanently prevent them from seceding.

Even justifying the bold strokes he took early in the war, Lincoln—who had called Congress into an emergency session to ratify his actions—continued to invoke an ethic of limitation. His focus was now on union. "Whatever concerns the whole [Union], should be confided to the whole—to the general government; while, whatever concerns *only* the State, should be left exclusively, to the State. This is all there is of original principle about it." Even when he suspended habeas corpus, permitting the indefinite detention of anti-Union agitators, Lincoln insisted to Congress that "[t]his authority has purposely been exercised but very sparingly."

Lincoln drew criticism from radical Republicans for his persistent caution on the issue of slavery. He revoked General John C. Frémont's order emancipating people enslaved by rebels in Missouri, the area of his command, in the fall of 1861 and did so again that winter, when General David Hunter issued a similar directive in several Southern states. Significantly, Lincoln acknowledged that in the latter case, he, like Hunter, was prudently balancing goods and evil. Hunter "expected more good, and less harm from the measure, than I could believe would follow." When the political authorities declared emancipation, he said in revoking Hunter's order, "it shall have become a necessity indispensable to the maintenance of the government...." But the essence of prudence is not, again, accession to circumstance but rather accommodation to it in pursuit of a long-range and rightful goal. Lincoln thus appealed to the border states in Hunter's command—"I now earnestly appeal, I do not argue"—"to make the arguments [for gradual emancipation] for yourselves. You can not if you would, be blind to the signs of the times. I beg of you a calm and enlarged consideration of them, ranging, if it may be, far above personal and partizan politics." Proponents of slavery, too, had to accommodate prudently to circumstance.

The following summer, seeking to balance his opposition to slavery with the vital need to hold the border states—again, union was a necessary predicate to ending slavery—Lincoln made a proposal for emancipating slaves by compensating their owners: "I do not speak of emancipation *at once*, but of a *decision* at once to emancipate *gradually*." In December 1862, he proposed a constitutional amendment to Congress that would have compensated states that chose to emancipate enslaved people by 1900. He explained to Congress that "[t]he proposed emancipation would shorten the war, perpetuate peace, insure [an] increase of population, and proportionately the wealth of the country," which would cover the cost of compensation. The only barriers to such a plan would be "the folly and evils of disunion" or a "long and exhausting war springing from the only great element of national discord among us." This "only" indicates that well into the war, Lincoln sought to limit the scope of dispute. Gradual emancipation accommodated the nation to the circumstances it faced. Lincoln sought to soothe Northern fears of an influx of freed African Americans by noting that the circumstances of gradual emancipation would remove the incentive for fleeing north. His reassurance was suggestively prudent, a reminder of Burke's rejection of abstract theory: "Again," Lincoln wrote to Congress, "as practice proves more than theory, in any case, has there been any irruption of colored people northward, because of the abolishment of slavery in this District [of Columbia] last spring?"

Perhaps Lincoln's most powerful statement of prudent accommodation to circumstance was contained in his September 1862 reply to Chicagoans who urged emancipation. Lincoln explained that he was often told that emancipation was God's will, though he wryly responded that if God were to reveal His will to anyone on the topic, he would hope it would be to the president whose duty was involved. But, and this is the crucial point about prudence: "These are not, however, the days of miracles, and I suppose it will be granted that I am not to expect a direct revelation. I must study the plain physical facts of the case, ascertain what is possible and learn what appears to be wise and right." Emancipation was right, but would not be wise under the circumstances, in which it would be unenforceable. "Would *my word* free the slaves, when I cannot even enforce the Constitution in the rebel States?" As late as April 1864, he told the Kentucky Unionist Albert G. Hodges that while he was "naturally anti-slavery" and that "[i]f slavery is not wrong, nothing is wrong" and "I can not remember when I did not

so think, and feel," the Constitution did not permit him "to practically
indulge my primary abstract judgment on the moral question of slavery."
Importantly, this was true "in ordinary *civil* administration" (emphasis
added), as opposed to military affairs.

Consequently, even when Lincoln resolved to issue the Emancipation
Proclamation, he waited until it was justifiable as a military necessity
and battlefield conditions made it enforceable—and even then he gave
the rebel states notice and the option to return to the Union. Still, there
was an unmistakable element of boldness in this prudence. He wrote to
General John A. McClernand in January 1863:

> After the commencement of hostilities I struggled nearly a year and a
> half to get along without touching the "institution"; and when finally I
> conditionally determined to touch it, I gave a hundred days fair notice of
> my purpose, to all the States and people, within which time they could
> have turned it wholly aside, by simply again becoming good citizens of
> the United States. They chose to disregard it, and I made the peremptory
> proclamation on what appeared to me to be a military necessity. And
> being made, it must stand.

That summer, even while maintaining his plan of gradual emancipation in
border states, he said the Emancipation Proclamation would stand where
it had been promulgated. "Those who shall have tasted actual freedom I
believe can never be slaves, or quasi slaves, again," he wrote to General
Stephen A. Hurlbut. Lincoln told the Maryland abolitionist John Cres-
well in March 1864 that while he had thought gradual emancipation
"would produce less confusion, and destitution," he would not object if
those who were better acquainted with and more interested in the subject
judged that immediate emancipation was preferable.

Lincoln's caution was likewise evident in his veto of a congressional
reconstruction plan in July 1864. His veto message said it had been presented to him less than an hour before the legislature adjourned and that
he was "unprepared, by a formal approval of this Bill, to be inflexibly committed to any single plan of restoration...."When he did propose terms of
reconstruction, they were magnanimous.

Still, his prudence, like Burke's, contained unmistakable elements of
boldness.

Boldness as Prudence

Traces of Lincoln's boldness were evident early in his career, as when he told Congress in 1848 that it was too risk-averse on internal improvements. The position of opponents of internal improvements, he argued, amounted to "Do nothing at all, lest you do something wrong." But it was the issue of slavery—the one that admitted, ultimately, no middle, the one that threatened to divide the national house against itself—that most called forth his assertive spirit. Lincoln wrote in an 1860 campaign biography that he had generally forsaken politics when the repeal of the Missouri Compromise "aroused him as he had never been before." We have already seen that Lincoln maintained his cautious, gradual posture during this time, even as he fixed his gaze on slavery's end. But as they had not at the time of the Lyceum Address, circumstances would increasingly call for boldness. Like Burke, Lincoln was innately cautious, in no small part because his Whig origins emphasized deliberation. But also like Burke, Lincoln's insightful judgment indicated when ultimate issues were at stake and when decisive action was the only means of resolving them. During the interregnum between his 1860 election and his 1861 inauguration, Lincoln wrote to his Secretary of State-designate, William H. Seward, that he remained "inflexible" on the question of slavery in territories. "I am for no compromise which *assists* or *permits* the extension of the institution on soil owned by the nation."

Circumstances would increasingly call for inflexibility. En route to the nation's capital to take office amid a cascade of seceding states, Lincoln grasped this, telling the New Jersey General Assembly that "the man does not live who is more devoted to peace than I am. None who would do more to preserve it. But it may be necessary to put the foot down firmly." It bears emphasis that he would put his foot down under conditions of necessity, as opposed to audacity and firmness for their own sake. Speaking at Independence Hall in Philadelphia during the same journey, he hoped the Union could be saved while preserving the Declaration's principle of equality. "But, if this country cannot be saved without giving up that principle—I was about to say I would rather be assassinated on this spot than to surrender it."

Lincoln persistently refused to recognize the legality or even the reality of secession. He never referred to the Southern confederacy as a nation and repeatedly refused to receive offers of peace while Jefferson Davis cast himself and his negotiators as agents of a foreign power. In his First Inaugural, Lincoln thus said that "in view of the Constitution and the laws, the Union *is* unbroken; and, to the extent of my ability, I shall take care, as the Constitution itself expressly enjoins upon me, that the laws of the Union be faithfully executed in all the States" (emphasis added). Similarly, he later told Samuel P. Lee of the Navy Department, who had transmitted a message from Alexander H. Stephens, the Confederate vice president and an old congressional colleague of Lincoln, that as president he would not receive any message "when offered, as in this case, in terms assuming the independence of the so-called Confederate States...."

Facing the attack on Ft. Sumter while Congress was out of session, Lincoln ordered a blockade, enlisted soldiers and, most controversially, suspended the writ of habeas corpus. The latter in particular raised cries of tyranny, but Lincoln refused to apologize for his decisiveness, later responding to New York critics by noting how much blood could have been saved had Confederate generals been detained before the rebellion, when it was known they would join it. "Every one of them, if arrested, would have been discharged on *habeas corpus* were the writ allowed to operate. In view of these and similar cases, I think the time not unlikely to come when I shall be blamed for having made too few arrests rather than too many."

Constitutional scholars have generally excused these measures as legal because they were necessary for national preservation. But necessity does not make constitutionality; rather, prudence understands when one must step temporarily outside the channels of normal law. It was the nature of Lincoln's prudence to see his war measures as what Burke would call exceptions from which general rules could not be drawn. Lincoln convened Congress as quickly as was practicable to ratify his actions. Explaining his reasoning, Lincoln told legislators that "no choice was left but to call out the war power of the Government; and so to resist force, employed for its destruction, by force, for its preservation." Lincoln explained that he had to balance the propriety of legal ambiguities like the suspension of habeas corpus against "the whole of the laws," which "were being resisted, and failing of execution, in nearly one-third of the States." This is the language of a statesman recognizing an ultimate issue, much like Burke had in condemning peace with the French revolutionaries. It was as prudent to act firmly during the rebellion as it had been to act cautiously before the war. Lincoln changed tacks to accommodate himself to circumstance.

He identified this ultimate issue in his famous August 1862 letter to the editor Horace Greeley: "My paramount object in this struggle is to save the Union, and is *not* either to save or to destroy slavery. If I could save the Union without freeing *any* slave I would do it, and if I could save it by freeing *all* the slaves I would do it; and if I could save it by freeing some and leaving others alone I would also do that." Note the prudence involved in choosing among these alternatives according to conditions; the Emancipation Proclamation reflected such a prudential calculation and resolved it on the side of boldness. It is equally important to recall that, while union was the ultimate goal, it was also a precondition to ending slavery. Later that year, proposing compensated emancipation by constitutional amendment, he wrote to Congress of the ultimate nature of the issues at stake:

> Fellow-citizens, we cannot escape history. We of this Congress and this administration, will be remembered in spite of ourselves. No personal significance, or insignificance, can spare one or another of us. The fiery trial through which we pass, will light us down, in honor or dishonor, to the latest generation. We *say* we are for the Union. The world will not forget that we say this. We know how to save the Union. The world knows we do know how to save it. We—even we *here*—hold the power, and bear the responsibility. In *giving* freedom to the *slave*, we *assure* freedom to the *free*—honorable alike in what we give, and what we preserve. We shall nobly save, or meanly lose, the last best hope of earth. Other means may succeed; this could not fail. The way is plain, peaceful, generous, just—a way which, if followed, the world will forever applaud, and God must forever bless.

Lincoln did not flinch from the responsibility he identified. Even noting that many members of Congress were more experienced than he was in public affairs, he accepted the mantle of command: "Yet I trust that in view of the great responsibility resting upon me, you will perceive no want of respect to yourselves, in any undue earnestness I may seem to display." The situation was "piled high with difficulty," he continued, "and we must rise—with the occasion." Again, though, we see attention to circumstance, which demanded boldness, rather than audacity for its own sake: "As our case is new, so we must think anew, and act anew. We must disenthrall ourselves [from 'the dogmas of the quiet past'], and then we shall save our country." Using exactly the same analogy Burke had deployed with respect to American taxation, Lincoln told Albert G. Hodges that it was absurd to say the nation should perish to preserve the letter of the Constitution. "By general law life and limb must be protected; yet often a limb must be amputated to save a life; but a life is never wisely given to save a limb." Even here, Lincoln chose between what he recognized as competing evils: skirting the edges of the Constitution on the one hand, and losing the Union on the other.

The ultimate nature of the stakes made bold strokes imperative, as a result of which Lincoln was profoundly vexed by the inactivity and risk aversion of his early commanders. In October 1862, he wrote Union General George B. McClellan that "[y]ou remember my speaking to you of what I called your over-cautiousness. Are you not over-cautious when you assume that you can not do what the enemy is constantly doing? Should you not claim to be at least his equal in prowess, and act upon the claim?" Caution, it bears emphasis, was not the problem; excess caution was. As Lincoln's confidence in his military judgment grew, he dismissed the vain McClellan, replacing him eventually—after a series of commanders whose over-caution also distressed him—with Ulysses S. Grant, whose obstinate daring and relentless activity endeared him to the president.

Perhaps Lincoln's boldest move was his insistence on proceeding with the 1864 presidential election even when it appeared that McClellan, by then the Democratic nominee, would win and, as a result, the Union might be lost. Upon Lincoln's decisive victory, which followed a reversal of battlefield misfortunes, he told serenaders at the White House that holding an election in the midst of a Civil War had proved to the world that a government could be strong enough to maintain both liberty and order even during crises. "[T]he election was a necessity. We can not have free government without elections; and if the rebellion could force us to forego, or postpone a national election, it might fairly claim to have already conquered and ruined us." He proceeded with a prudential assessment of the political strife the nation had just survived: "The strife of the election is but human-nature practically applied to the facts of the case. What has occurred in this case, must ever recur in similar cases. Human-nature will not change."

Lincoln's annual message to Congress that December remained resolute in the face of ultimate questions.

> On careful consideration of all the evidence accessible it seems to me that no attempt at negotiation with the insurgent leader could result in any good. He would accept nothing short of severance of the Union—precisely what we will not and cannot give. His declarations to this effect are explicit and oft-repeated. He does not attempt to deceive us. He affords us no excuse to deceive ourselves. He cannot voluntarily reaccept the Union; we cannot voluntarily yield it. Between him and us the issue is distinct, simple, and inflexible. It is an issue which can only be tried by war, and decided by victory.

We shall have occasion in Chapter 4 to consider Lincoln's greatest speech, the Second Inaugural, more fully. In a commanding analysis, Reinhold Niebuhr's *The Irony of American History* considers it a masterwork of prudent rhetoric. It is, but part of that prudence is the boldness with which Lincoln, on the cusp of complete triumph, extended magnanimity to the enemy even while stating principle clearly. "Both read the same Bible, and pray to the same God; and each invokes His aid against the other. It may seem strange that any men should dare to ask a just God's assistance in wringing their bread from the sweat of other men's faces; but let us judge not that we be not judged." Perhaps even more boldly, Lincoln attributed the war to Divine wrath directed against the entire nation, not just the rebellious South. This language is damning to North and South alike:

> If we shall suppose that American Slavery is one of those offences which, in the providence of God, must needs come, but which, having continued through His appointed time, He now wills to remove, and that He gives to both North and South, this terrible war, as the woe due to those by whom the offence came, shall we discern therein any departure from those divine attributes which the believers in a Living God always ascribe to Him? Fondly do we hope—fervently do we pray—that this mighty scourge of war may speedily pass away. Yet, if God wills that it

continue, until all the wealth piled by the bond-man's two hundred and fifty years of unrequited toil shall be sunk, and until every drop of blood drawn with the lash, shall be paid by another drawn with the sword, as was said three thousand years ago, so still it must be said "the judgments of the Lord, are true and righteous altogether."

Lincoln was aware of this rhetorical risk. He wrote to the New York political operative Thurlow Weed afterward that he expected history, but not his contemporaries, to receive the address well: "Men are not flattered by being shown that there has been a difference of purpose between the Almighty and them. To deny it, however, in this case, is to deny that there is a God governing the world. It is a truth which I thought needed to be told; and as whatever of humiliation there is in it, falls most directly on myself, I thought others might afford for me to tell it."

Generational Change

There is a final dimension of Lincoln's prudence that merits attention, and the legacy of the Second Inaugural illustrates it. Lincoln, like Burke, saw political life transcending generations. We have already seen this emerge in his desire for emancipation to proceed in the border states gradually over a period of decades, almost certainly beyond the scope of Lincoln's own life. The Lyceum Address, similarly, said that to violate the law and thus undermine the regime was "to trample on the blood of his father, and to tear the character of his own, and his children's liberty." Generational vision was the work of great souls: Lincoln had recognized as much in telling the Washington Temperance Society that appealing to a distant future would not persuade alcoholics to give up drink.

Lincoln was such a soul, and it is evident in another means of generational, indeed timeless, influence, one in which Lincoln excelled as much as any craftsman in the language: writing. Compare his formulation of intergenerational communication in his 1859 "Lecture on Discoveries and Inventions" to Burke's understanding of the social contract as binding "those who are living, those who are dead, and those who are to be born":

Writing—the art of communicating thoughts to the mind, through the eye—is the great invention of the world. Great in the astonishing range of analysis and combination which necessarily underlies the most crude and general conception of it—great, very great in enabling us to converse with the dead, the absent, and the unborn, at all distances of time and space....

Lincoln's ideas transcended time and space. But there was a prudent dimension in his, and Burke's, concepts of reason itself—concepts that differ in fundamental respects but share the quality of prudence.

CHAPTER THREE

℘ ℘

Sophisters, Economists, and Calculators

Burke on Reason and Revelation

In the 1750s, Burke, then in his 20s, jotted notes on the topic of "Philosophy and Learning" in a notebook that was not published for another two centuries. "It signifies much less what we read than how we read, and with a view to what end," he wrote. "To study only for its own sake is a fruitless labor; to learn only to be learned is moving in a strange Circle. The End of learning is not knowledge but virtue; as the End of all speculation should be practice of one sort or another." Over his life, Burke would develop this theme into what might be called a theory of reason with an ironic twist: Self-contained reason tended to be difficult to contain. Grounding the abstract in the concrete—as in "practice" in the passage from the notebook—cabined it. Abstraction was arrogant, while practice drew on what Burke would later, in the *Reflections*, call "the general bank and capital of nations and of ages." The great Burke scholar Francis Canavan called this "political reason": a form of reason that understood the importance of the concrete over the abstract and, crucially, one that knew its own limits.

In the 1750s notebook, Burke consequently drew a contrast between those whose long course of study induces humility and uncertainty and those "who know nothing at all of Literature ... despise all the advantages

of Study in comparison of their own natural Genius."The opinion of the
first group "arises from depth of thought and humility; the other from
profound ignorance and the most intolerable pride."The reason of this
arrogant cohort was Cartesian in nature. Burke's "study" ranged the full
span of human experience as it was reflected through such prisms as
literature and history.

That is not to say Burke opposed the use of reason, and still less
that he endorsed the irrational. He was steeped in a classical education. "I do not vilify theory and speculation: no, because that would
be to vilify reason itself," he said in his 1782 speech on parliamentary
reform. "No,—whenever I speak against theory, I mean always a weak,
erroneous, fallacious, unfounded, or imperfect theory; and one of the
ways of discovering that it is a false theory is by comparing it with
practice."Theory was false if it corrupted practice, a species of Burke's
more general argument that theories should be assessed according to
their consequences. What Burke derided as "metaphysical politics" was
especially prone to fanaticism because its practitioners recognized no
boundaries to either their reasoning capacity or the realm of its applica-
bility. Consequently, Burke said in his reply to the Unitarians, "I never
govern myself, no *rational* man ever did govern himself, by abstractions
and universals" (emphasis added). That did not mean he repudiated
reason, "because I well know that under that name I should dismiss
principles," leaving politics "only a confused jumble of particular facts
and details, without the means of drawing out any sort of theoretical
or practical conclusion."

Metaphysical politicians, he told the sheriffs of Bristol, fell prey to
"shocking extremes provoking to extremes of another kind, [so] speculations are let loose as destructive to all authority, as the former are to all
freedom; and every government is called tyranny and usurpation which
is not formed on their fancies." Burke, addressing the American crisis,
distinguished between the British constitution and "the Constitution of
the British Empire."The latter's power of taxing its colonies was more
circumscribed. He was unsure whether that distinction would satisfy "a
refining speculatist or a factious demagogue," but it was sufficient "for
the ease and happiness of man." From the first to the last of Burke's
writings, this understanding of reason was grounded in humility and
moderation.

Speculative Politics

In *A Vindication of Natural Society*, Burke anonymously lampooned both the style and ideas of Lord Bolingbroke's romantic writings on man's unvarnished, natural state. In the preface to the 1756 printing, in which Burke acknowledged having written the essay, he noted the propensity of abstract reason to carry its audiences away in flights of utopian fancy. "This is the fairy land of philosophy," he wrote, proceeding to ask: "Even in matters which are, as it were, just within our reach, what would become of the world, if the practice of all moral duties, and the foundations of society, rested upon having their reasons made clear and demonstrative to every individual?" Burke's fear was that exposing political community to the cynical spirit of abstract philosophy would undermine it to the point of collapse. This kind of exposure was dangerous because metaphysics was better at criticism than construction: Its leveling force could destroy, but when it built, it did so either poorly or fanatically. Theoretical politics had an inherently destructive quality. Burke wrote in the *Reflections* that "If all the absurd theories of lawyers and divines were to vitiate the objects in which they are conversant, we should have no law and no religion left in the world." One reason was that reason could easily see the defects of the present while "criticism [was] almost baffled" in identifying the problems with hypothetical reforms.

For this reason, Burke told Parliament in a 1783 debate about reform of the British East India Company: "I feel an insuperable reluctance in giving my hand to destroy any established institution of government, upon a theory, however plausible it may be." Separately, in the 1782 speech on parliamentary reform, Burke explained that it was "a presumption in favor of any settled scheme of government against any untried project, that a nation has long existed and flourished under it." This excelled "any sudden and temporary arrangement by actual election," a formulation that suggests that what is sudden is likely to be temporary.

As Chapter 7 will show, the established governments Burke meant to defend had to be long established and therefore presumably indicative of the best accumulation of human wisdom over time. England provided a case in point. Its government was based on prescription, the Roman law of long usage. It was consequently the product of slow evolution. Thus Burke's suspicion of parliamentary reform in the 1782 speech: "A prescriptive government, such as ours, never was the work of any legislator, never was made upon any foregone theory. It seems to me a preposterous way of reasoning, and a perfect confusion of ideas, to take the theories which learned and speculative men have made from that government, and then, supposing it made on those theories which were made from it, to accuse the government as not corresponding with them."

In a 1769 essay defending a series of Whig positions, including those on parliamentary reform and American affairs, Burke declined to accept theoretical justifications for changing the basis of representation in the legislature. "Not that I mean to condemn such speculative inquiries concerning this great object of the national attention. They may tend to clear doubtful points, and possibly may lead, as they have often done, to real improvements. What I object to, is their introduction into a discourse relating to the immediate state of our affairs, and recommending plans of practical government." The purpose of attempting to apply these theories to practice, he continued, was simply "to raise discontent in the people of England...." It was possible, simply by attending to the facts of the case, to resolve such questions as whether America should be represented in Parliament "without agitating those vexatious questions, which in truth rather belong to metaphysics than politics, and which can never be moved without shaking the foundations of the best governments that have ever been constituted by human wisdom." Wisdom and prudence belonged to politics, speculation to philosophy.

Abstract speculations were apt to deceive those who indulged them. Thus, speaking on America, Burke told Parliament: "Whoever goes about to reason on any part of the policy of this country with regard to America, upon the mere abstract principles of government, or even upon those of our own ancient constitution, will be often misled," in no small part because the situation was "wholly new in the world" and "singular." Because there was no history on which to draw, measures on America could only be judged by the circumstances of the case. Burke granted that a conflict existed between American freedom and the rights of British imperial rule. What he denied was that abstract philosophy, as opposed to prudence, could resolve it: "Whether all this can be reconciled in legal speculation, is a matter of no consequence. It is reconciled in policy: and politics ought to be adjusted, not to human reasonings, but to human nature; of which the reason is but a part, and by no means the greatest part."

Human nature was a grounding, limiting principle—a principle of prudence—whereas untethered speculation was prone to abuse. In the *Reflections*, Burke observed of the philosophical doctrine of "the rights of man" that "[t]he pretended rights of these theorists are all extremes; and in proportion as they are metaphysically true, they are morally and politically false." The formulation suggests both that metaphysics tended toward the extreme and that there was a difference in kind between metaphysical truth on the one hand and moral and political truth on the other. Speaking on American taxation, Burke said the Americans would accede to taxation of their global trade "if they are not pushed with too much logic and too little sense...." In 1792, as he retreated from public life, he complained to his parliamentary colleague William Weddell of the Whig leaders who had become enchanted with the French Revolution: They were "sublime Metaphysicians; and the horrible consequences produced by their Speculations affect them not at all. They only ask whether the proposition be true?—Whether it produces good or evil is no part of their concern."

The *Letters on a Regicide Peace* made a similar point: "Matters of prudence are under the dominion of circumstances, and not of logical analogies. It is absurd to take it otherwise." Placing prudence under the superintendence of logic was, significantly, itself logically "absurd." That was simply not the realm in which prudence operated. In the speech on American taxation, Burke said of a parliamentary colleague: "He asserts, that retrospect is not wise; and the proper, the only proper subject of inquiry, is 'not how we got into this difficulty, but how we are to get out of it.' In other words, we are, according to him, to consult our invention, and to reject our experience. The mode of deliberation he recommends is diametrically opposite to every rule of reason and every principle of good sense established amongst mankind." Accommodation to circumstance was not a substitute for reason but rather an exercise of it.

The quest for philosophical precision in politics, Burke wrote, was both doomed and dangerous. There could be, for example, no exact formula to determine when revolution was justified, as he wrote in the *Reflections*: "The speculative line of demarcation, where obedience ought to end and resistance must begin, is faint, obscure, and not easily definable." Revolution must be a matter of necessity so clear as not to require deliberation. But it is important to note that these faint lines did not mean there was no difference between right and wrong. Burke explained in *Thoughts on the Cause of the Present Discontents*:

> No lines can be laid down for civil or political wisdom. They are a matter incapable of exact definition. But, though no man can draw a stroke between the confines of day and night, yet light and darkness are upon the whole tolerably distinguishable. Nor will it be impossible for a prince to find out such a mode of government, and such persons to administer it, as will give a great degree of content to his people; without any curious and anxious research for that abstract, universal, perfect harmony, which while he is seeking, he abandons those means of ordinary tranquility which are in his power without any research at all.

Weaver's criticism of Burke's rejection of speculation as a principle of action, which the former reduces to mere consequentialism, substantially overlooks the philosophical grounding of his critique of philosophical politics. This is true in three respects. First, in *Discontents*, Burke linked the statesman's vocation with the philosopher's: "It is the business of the speculative philosopher to mark the proper ends of government. It is the business of the politician, who is the philosopher in action, to find out proper means towards those ends, and to employ them with effect." This is the classical definition of prudence. It was in the choice of means, not ends, that speculation was dangerous. The statesman was not opposed to reason, but it was reason of a particular type. The role of the politician, as "the philosopher in action," was to apply Canavan's "political reason." When applied to the choice of means, political reason was a confining principle, whereas imaginative or speculative politics was unbound. Second, accommodation to circumstance is a concession to the complexity of society, a reality that political reason ascertains. Burke said in reply to the Unitarians: "Circumstances are infinite, are infinitely combined, are variable and transient: he who does not take them into consideration is not erroneous, but stark mad...he is metaphysically mad."

Finally, we have already seen that his moderation was principled, not a matter of consequentialism or convenience. Speculative politics tended inescapably toward fanaticism, a position Burke developed most fully in his reaction to the French Revolution but of which he was aware well before. His speech on American taxation urged Parliament: "If you apprehend that on a concession [to the colonies] you shall be pushed by metaphysical process to the extreme lines, and argued out of your whole authority, my advice is this: when you have recovered your old, your strong, your tenable position, then face about,—stop short,—do nothing more,—reason not at all,—oppose the ancient policy and practice of the empire as a rampart against the speculations of innovators on both sides of the question...." We have already encountered Burke's view of "innovators"; it is significant in this context that he sets up "ancient policy and practice" to oppose them.

A precision was accessible to metaphysics that was wholly unsuited to the moving pieces and infinite complexity of political life. In *Discontents*, Burke wrote that "example" was "the only argument of effect in *civil* life..." (emphasis added). He told Parliament in the "Speech on Conciliation with the Colonies": "Aristotle, the great master of reasoning, cautions us, and with great weight and propriety, against this species of delusive geometrical accuracy in moral arguments, as the most fallacious of all sophistry." In his writings on France, the Revolution's division of the country's ancient provinces into newly and precisely drawn districts based on geometry rather than affinity became a symbol of this vain and fruitless search for formulaic politics. These divisions required no prudence, only the talents of a surveyor. But, Burke wrote in the *Reflections*, the surveyors soon discovered that "in politics the most fallacious of all things was geometrical demonstration." Similarly: "The legislators who framed the ancient republicans knew that their business was too arduous to be accomplished with no better apparatus than the metaphysics of an undergraduate and the mathematics of an exciseman."

This was a concession to, in fact an embrace of, the diversity and complexity of actual political life. Formulas were universal, whereas the variegation of political life made constitutions specific to political communities. Moreover, even within those communities, formulas were unsuited to the complexity of human beings living in society. Importantly, this universalism naturally bred fanaticism and was impossible to confine to national borders, which was why Burke saw Jacobinism as uniquely dangerous and imperialistic. In *Thoughts on French Affairs*, he compared it to the Protestant Reformation, "the last revolution of dogma and theory which has happened in Europe," the effects of which were felt across the continent regardless of national borders because they made universal claims grounded in the intellect.

In his famous soliloquy on Marie Antoinette, Burke wrote: "I thought ten thousand swords must have leaped from their scabbards to avenge even a look that threatened her with insult. But the age of chivalry is gone. That of sophisters, economists, and calculators has succeeded; and the glory of Europe is extinguished forever." This opposition of chivalry—an affective virtue—to "economists and calculators" suggests the devastating effects of displacing the warmth of human feeling with the coldness of logic divorced from circumstance. In the connection between "economists and calculators" and "sophists," we again see that philosophical politics is itself unphilosophical: It is a breed of sophism, the classical rhetorical trick of making the weaker argument appear to be the stronger. The use of sophism, in turn, suggests there was in fact a stronger argument, a deeper truth, to contrast with the reductive rhetoric of calculation. The deeper truth was political reason: the application of profound principle to concrete circumstance. The economists and calculators were neither profound—they merely tabulated—nor concrete.

The Sublime and Beautiful reached a similar conclusion: "To multiply principles for every different appearance is useless, and unphilosophical too in a high degree." The *Reflections*, exploring a similar theme, said that the mistakes of the prudent were more forgivable than those of speculative innovators:

> We must always see with a pity not unmixed with respect the errors of those who are timid and doubtful of themselves with regard to points wherein the happiness of mankind is concerned. But in [the French revolutionaries] there is nothing of the tender parental solicitude which fears to cut up the infant for the sake of an experiment. In the vastness of their promises and the confidence of their predictions they far outdo all the boasting of empirics. The arrogance of their pretensions in a manner provokes and challenges us to an inquiry into their foundation.

Commending prudence to Parliament with respect to American affairs, Burke urged his colleagues to "consider distinctly the true nature and the peculiar circumstances of the object which we have before us...." This application of a thing's "true nature" to "peculiar circumstance" was essential to Burkean prudence, which linked circumstance to the absolute. He continued: "[A]fter all our struggle, whether we will or not, we must govern America according to that nature and to those circumstances, and not according to our own imaginations, not according to abstract ideas of right, by no means according to mere general theories of government, the resort to which appears to me, in our present situation, no better than arrant trifling."

Speculation could be merely errant, but it might also be positively dangerous, and practitioners of what Burke derided as "literary politics" were especially prone to it. The *Reflections* noted that "[m]en of letters, fond of distinguishing themselves, are rarely averse to innovation." Their motive, in other words, was corrupt and selfish. The *Reflections* emphasized the point more than once, as in, "A spirit of innovation is generally the result of a selfish temper and confined views." Thus the *Appeal*: "[The Jacobins] build their politics, not on convenience, but on truth; and they profess to conduct men to certain happiness by the assertion of their undoubted rights. With them there is no compromise. All other governments are usurpations, which justify and even demand resistance." Theoreticians were inherently given to extremes, Burke wrote in the *Reflections*: "These professors, finding their extreme principles not applicable to cases which call only for a qualified, or, as I may say, civil and legal resistance, in such cases employ no resistance at all. It is with them a war or a revolution, or it is nothing."

A speculator convinced he has laid hold of the whole truth has no reason to moderate his views; such will even seem unreasonable, even heretical, to him. Neither will he think twice of sacrificing individuals to something as grand and abstract as the truth or, in the slogan of the Revolution, "Liberty, Equality, Fraternity"—objectives so abstract that, as Martin Diamond has noted, it was impossible to say definitively when or whether they had been achieved. Divorced from circumstance, such slogans could become murderous—were, in fact, likely to be so. Fraternity, for example, descended into what the French playwright and wit Nicolas Chamfort called "Be my brother or I will kill you." Speculation accomplished what Burke, in the *Regicide Peace*, called a "hocus-pocus" by which the English ministry claimed it was negotiating with territorial France, when in fact it was dealing with philosophical Jacobinism. This was all the more dangerous because Burke wrote of a rising Jacobin faction inside

English borders. It was the nature of reason that these ideas, as opposed to traditions, could not be confined to national borders.

Speculative politics was also over-confident in its ability to predict the consequences of its ideas and then unwilling to adjust when those consequences emerged. This is the law of unintended consequences that is so central to Burke's conservatism. In March 1757, he wrote in the only recently discovered and published note *Considerations on a Militia*: "When Men already in a good Condition, think of innovating in any Respect, they have a Course of which they know the advantages, so as to push them to their Utmost. They leave a Course of which they know the disadvantages, so as to know the best Methods of contending against them: they leave this for another the good of which is uncertain & many of whose Evil Consequences lying in the womb of time tis impossible to know." Simple abstractions could not be mapped onto the complexity of society.

Writing to the sheriffs of Bristol, Burke clearly contrasted prudence with metaphysics: "There are people who have split and anatomized the doctrine of free government, as if it were an abstract question concerning metaphysical liberty and necessity, and not a matter of moral prudence and natural feeling." This language bears close observation. The philosophers have "split and anatomized" government as an abstract question, taking it apart into pieces, which suggests a contrast with the "enlarged" and "combining mind" that Burke has previously told us characterizes prudence. "Metaphysical liberty and necessity" are opposed to "moral prudence and natural feeling." There is no prudence in metaphysics because its nature is to seek truth to its utmost limits, whereas limitation—a concession to the complexity of society and the limits of human wisdom—is an essential feature of political reason. Responding to the petition of the Unitarian Society, Burke thus told Parliament, "A statesman differs from a professor in an university: the latter has only the general view of society; the former, the statesman, has a number of circumstances to combine with those general ideas, and to take into his consideration."

The irony was that the philosophers on whom the Revolutionary French drew did not even mean to be taken literally. The *Reflections* explained that "the paradoxes of eloquent writers, brought forth purely as a sport of fancy, to try their talents, to rouse attention, and excite surprise, are taken up by these gentlemen, not in the spirit of the original authors, as means of cultivating their taste and improving their style: these paradoxes become with them serious grounds of action, upon which they proceed in regulating the most important concerns of the state." Rousseau, the patron saint of the Revolution, would, were he "alive, and in one of his lucid intervals…be shocked at the practical frenzy of his scholars, who in their paradoxes are servile imitators, and even in their incredulity discover an implicit faith."

"The Dominion of Circumstance"

What Weaver dismissed as Burke's unprincipled "argument from circumstance" was actually an argument from principled moderation, which unbridled speculation threatened to derange. In a famous passage from the *Reflections*, Burke wrote that he loved "a manly, moral, regulated liberty" as much as any supporter of the French Revolution. "But I cannot stand forward, and give praise or blame to anything which relates to human actions and human concerns on a simple view of the object, as it stands stripped of every relation, in all the nakedness and solitude of metaphysical abstraction. Circumstances (which with some gentlemen pass for nothing) give in reality to every political principle its distinguishing color and discriminating effect. The circumstances are what render every civil and political scheme beneficial or noxious to mankind." He explained in his reply to the Unitarian Society: "A statesman, never losing sight of principles, is to be guided by circumstances; and judging contrary to the exigencies of the moment, he may ruin his country forever…. The first question a good statesman would ask himself, therefore, would be, How and in what circumstances do you find the society? and to act upon them." This could serve as a working definition of prudence. Burke reminds us that a statesman is always focused on principles, but must adjust to circumstances in choosing the means to attain them.

For this reason, Parliament's abstract reasons for insisting on England's right to tax the colonies were irrelevant to Burke. He told Parliament: "The question with me, is not whether you have a right to render your people miserable, but whether it is not your interest to make them happy." Likewise, he was "resolved this day to have nothing at all to do with the question of the right of taxation." He allowed that "gentlemen of profound learning are fond of displaying it on this profound object. But my consideration is narrow, confined, and wholly limited to the policy of the question." It is significant that while prudence was "enlarged," Burke's considerations on an abstract question of parliamentary authority were "confined."

Circumstantial reasoning helped to limit, as we shall shortly see, abstract flights of philosophy. In the speech on the Unitarian petition, Burke raised the question of whether it would be reasonable to deny something "right in itself" demanded by one religious sect because it might lead to improper demands from others. "Abstractedly speaking, there can be no doubt that this question ought to be decided in the negative. But as no moral questions are ever abstract questions, this, before I judge upon any abstract proposition, must be embodied in circumstances; for, since things are right or wrong, morally speaking, only by their relation and connection with other things, this very question of what it is politically right to grant depends upon this relation to its effects."

This "relation and connection" is the work of the "combining mind" that we have seen is part of prudence, and it is inseparable from the grounding, limiting condition of circumstance. It is for this reason that the circumstantial reasoning Weaver dismisses as unconservative is actually part of the essence of a politics that conserves by basing shared life on the concrete rather than the rootless abstract. Circumstantial politics is grounded not just in moderation but also in humility, especially about the ability of theory to forecast the infinitely complex workings of political society. Burke said in the Warren Hastings trial: "The best way of showing that a theoretical system is bad is to show the practical mischiefs that it produces: because a thing may look specious in theory, and yet be ruinous in practice; a thing may look evil in theory, and yet be in its practice excellent. Here a thing in theory, stated by Mr. Hastings to be productive of much good, is in reality productive of all those horrible mischiefs I have stated."

Burke's 1769 pamphlet criticized what he believed were fantastical plans to call Americans to England to serve in Parliament: "Enough of this visionary union; in which much extravagance appears without any fancy, and the judgment is shocked without anything to refresh the imagination. It looks as if the author had dropped down from the moon, without any knowledge of the general nature of this globe, of the general nature of its inhabitants, without the least acquaintance with the affairs of this country." The statesman's business was not the theoretical ideal but rather the practical reality. In 1780, Burke presented a plan to Parliament to reform the economic benefits that flowed to the court faction. He cautioned against theoretical idealism:

> I know it is common for men to say, that such and such things are perfectly right, very desirable,—but that, unfortunately, they are not practicable. Oh, no, Sir! no! Those things which are not practicable are not desirable. There is nothing in the world really beneficial that does not lie within the reach of an informed understanding and a well-directed pursuit. There is nothing that God has judged good for us that He has not given us the means to accomplish, both in the natural and the moral world. If we cry, like children, for the moon, like children we must cry on.

Burke likewise warned Parliament not to be absorbed by its own pride in dealing with the Americans. "They tell you, Sir, that your dignity is tied to it. I know not how it happens, but this dignity of yours is a terrible incumbrance to you; for it has of late been ever at war with your interest, your equity, and every idea of your policy." The use of equity in this passage is suggestive. Equity is the legal principle that relaxes the universal rigor of law in light of individual circumstance. In this case, Burke argued it was reckless to push the theoretical right to the colonies to its extremes simply to make a point, when the practical consequences of doing so would be destructive.

Concrete circumstance was the direct alternative to the boundless risks of abstract theory. In one sense, theory could become vapid, as in the case of Richard Price, the English cleric and supporter of the French Revolution whom Burke criticized in the *Reflections*: "It is somewhat remarkable that this reverend divine should be so earnest for setting up new churches, and so perfectly indifferent concerning the doctrine which may be taught in them. His zeal is of a curious character. It is not for the propagation of his own opinions, but of any opinions. It is not for the diffusion of truth, but for the spreading of contradiction. Let the noble teachers but dissent, it is no matter from whom or from what." But even this vacuity was perilous because it was unmoored.

Speaking to conciliation with the colonies, Burke said he had "in general no very exalted opinion of the virtue of paper government, nor of any Politics in which the plan is to be wholly separated from the execution." The question regarding the colonists was not who did what to whom or who did it first. "[T]he question is not, whether their spirit deserves praise or blame,—what, in the name of God, shall we do with it? You have before you the object, such as it is,—with all its glories, with all its imperfections on its head." This grounding in circumstance is inseparable from the prudent statesman's choice between evils. Parliament knew this, he noted, since it had decided to suspend the Constitution of Massachusetts, the seedbed of rebellion, but not those of other states: "Ideas of prudence and accommodation to circumstances prevent you from taking away the charters of Connecticut and Rhode Island, as you have taken away that of Massachusetts Colony.... The same reasons of prudence and accommodation have weight with me in restoring the charter of Massachusetts Bay." Similarly, discussing India in 1783, he remarked that no one would wish for the situation the British Empire faced, but it was reality and demanded accommodation: "The situation of man is the preceptor of his duty."

Attention to circumstance also allows the prudent statesman to change course, but not ultimate principle, in light of conditions on the ground. Writing to the sheriffs of Bristol, Burke said Parliament should have changed its mind on the prudence of taxing the colonies for a simple reason: "Because a different state of things requires a different conduct." He told the Irish political leader Sir Hercules Langrishe in a 1792 letter that conditions on the ground in Ireland must dictate English policy there. But he denied that this belief undercut the ends toward which prudence was directed: "I perfectly agree with you, that times and circumstances, considered with reference to the public, ought very much to govern our conduct,—though I am far from slighting, when applied with discretion to those circumstances, general principles and maxims of policy."

Burke believed circumstantial considerations protected against utopianism while disregard of them risked abuse. The statesman who refused to bend theory to circumstance must instead bend human nature to theory. In 1793, Burke wrote his son Richard, who had gone to Ireland as an advocate for Catholic suffrage: "The legislature of Ireland, like all legislatures, ought to frame its laws to suit the people and the circumstances of the country, and not any longer to make it their whole business to force the nature, the temper, and the inveterate habits of a nation to a conformity to speculative systems concerning any kind of laws." An attempt to wrench human nature into a theoretical mold, as the French experiment showed, inevitably required brutality. By contrast, Burke wrote in *Regicide Peace*, in all the "old countries" of Christendom, "the state has been made to the people, and not the people conformed to the state."

Circumstances equally served to expose faulty theories. Thus his 1791 *Letter to a Member of the National Assembly*: "Proceeding, therefore, as we are obliged to proceed,—that is, upon an hypothesis that we address rational men,—can false political principles be more effectually exposed than by demonstrating that they lead to consequences directly inconsistent with and subversive of the arrangements grounded upon them?" He replied to those who sought reform of the British constitution in 1782: "To those who say it is a bad one, I answer, Look to its effects. In all moral machinery, the moral results are its test." That is, the results, like the machinery, pertain to morality and are consequently the best means of evaluating it: Moral machinery that produced immoral results would be pointless.

"The Moral Constitution of the Heart"

In his intellectual biography of the first half of Burke's career, David Bromwich observes: "In a sentimental age, he stood for the integrity of ideas. In a class distinguished by its faith in reason, he stood for the inseparable value of feeling." Yuval Levin notes that this emphasis on "emotional, not only rational, edification and instruction…would become crucial to [Burke's] insistence that government must function in accordance with the forms and traditions of a society's life and not only abstract principles of justice," while Richard Bourke emphasizes Burke's "persistent aversion to stoic teaching." Feeling, being more innate to man and more grounded in his nature, was less prone to extremes than untethered reason.

In his most self-consciously philosophical tract, *A Philosophical Inquiry into the Origin of Our Ideas of the Sublime and Beautiful*, Burke wrote that sympathy was the faculty by which "we enter into the concerns of others; that we are moved as they are moved, and are never suffered to be indifferent spectators of almost anything which men can do or suffer." *The*

Reflections compared sentiments to "the moral constitution of the heart" and regretted that the European tradition of chivalry—characterized by "pleasing illusions which made power gentle and obedience liberal"—was "to be dissolved by this new conquering empire of light and reason." In one of his most suggestive phrases, Burke proceeded to refer to these illusions as the products of a "moral imagination": "All the decent drapery of life is to be rudely torn off. All the superadded ideas, furnished from the wardrobe of a moral imagination, which the heart owns and the understanding ratifies, as necessary to cover the defects of our naked, shivering nature, and to raise it to dignity in our own estimation, are to be exploded, as a ridiculous, absurd, and antiquated fashion."

The moral imagination is among the most complicated ideas in the Burkean corpus. It refers partly to a capacity to project oneself into the sufferings and situations of others, but it is far richer than empathy. Its association with mystery is suggested by the fact that it supplies a "decent drapery of life," one that covers the sharper edges of political and social life and is to be "torn off" by the harsh edges of rationalism. This imagination, Irving Babbitt teaches, enables Burke to mediate a "religiously grounded" liberty humanistically. Crucially, this moral imagination was "own[ed]" by the heart but "ratifie[d]" by "the understanding." Feeling was entirely reconcilable with reason. The key feature of moral imagination was that, especially as reason underlay it, it drew people closer together, whereas speculative politics led to abstractions that caused people not only to spurn sympathy but actively to turn on one another. Ian Crowe has equally emphasized Burke's "historical" or "Whig" imagination, which enabled him to discern "a sort of collective memory" in the British con-stitutional experience rather than being locked into discrete expressions of positive law.

In the 1769 pamphlet, Burke linked feeling and principle, addressing those who spurned personal loyalty in politics. "Frequently relinquishing one set of men and adopting another, they grow into a total indifference to human feeling, as they had before to moral obligation; until at length, no one original impression remains upon their minds: every principle is obliterated; every sentiment effaced." Both principle *and* sentiment are endangered by this kind of disloyalty. These are complementary rather than competing values. Burke's evocative description in the *Reflections* of the events of October 6, 1789, when a mob drove the royal family from

Versailles to Paris, suggests that some natural human sympathy for the degradation of the great might have accomplished the restraint that philosophical politics repudiated. Reason and feeling were linked once more: "In events like these our passions instruct our reason." He went further in the *Appeal*, arguing that reason was inherently able to justify anything, including the destruction of a grand monarchy. "With such things before our eyes, our feelings contradict our theories; and when this is the case, the feelings are true, and the theory is false." The import of this striking formulation is that feelings, being more natural and innate, are both more trustworthy than untethered reason and can exceed rational conclusions even by the criterion of "truth."

Burke thus counseled Parliament to be attentive to American sentiment on taxation: "No man ever doubted that the commodity of tea could bear an imposition of three-pence. But no commodity will bear three-pence, or will bear a penny, when the general feelings of men are irritated, and two millions of people are resolved not to pay." In this sense, accommodation to feeling overlapped with accommodation to circumstance. Feeling was also a means of drawing people closer together by means of sympathy. For this reason, Burke's 1785 parliamentary speech on the Nabob of Arcot's debts regretted that the affairs of India seemed so foreign to the British: "I confess, I wish that some more feeling than I have yet observed for the sufferings of our fellow-creatures and fellow-subjects in that oppressed part of the world had manifested itself in any one quarter of the kingdom, or in any one large description of men."

Unbridled reason, by contrast, could extinguish human sympathy and furnish its own reasons for barbarism. Burke wrote in the *Reflections* of the Revolutionary French: "Justifying perfidy and murder for public benefit, public benefit would soon become the pretext, and perfidy and murder the end,—until rapacity, malice, revenge, and fear more dreadful than revenge, could satiate their insatiable appetites. Such must be the consequences of losing, in the splendor of these triumphs of the rights of men, all natural sense of wrong and right." This "natural sense" was inborn, so that the British "preserve the whole of our feelings still native and entire, unsophisticated by pedantry and infidelity. We have real hearts of flesh and blood beating in our bosoms." Significantly, all unnatural feelings were "false and spurious...." The British, the *Reflections* continued, "are generally men of untaught feelings...." "Untaught" here is suggestive. Feelings were natural to men; unlike political speculation, they did not need to be invented or imposed. Feelings—again, ratified by the under-standing—were in a sense superior to what Michael Oakeshott called "Rationalism." Note the difference between "knowing" and "feeling" in this passage from the *Reflections*: "We know, and, *what is better*, we feel inwardly, that religion is the basis of civil society, and the source of all good, and of all comfort" (emphasis added).

Conversely, moral feeling could protect against the abuses of reason. The French *philosophes*, Burke wrote in the *Appeal*, could not "take the moral sympathies of the human mind along with them, in abstractions separated from the good or evil condition of the state, from the quality of actions, and the character of the actors." Moral feeling was a princi-ple of limitation, unbounded reason a principle of extremes. He wrote in the *Appeal*: "It must always have been discoverable by persons of reflection, but it is now obvious to the world, that a theory concerning government may become as much a cause of fanaticism as a dogma in religion. There is a boundary to men's passions, when they act from feeling; none when they are under the influence of imagination." Feeling was also what Burke called a "cementing" principle between men, so he was displeased in writing his *Letter to a Member of the National Assembly* in 1791 that "[b]enevolence to the whole species, and want of feeling for every individual with whom the professors come into contact, form the character of the new philosophy."

Burke on Revelation

For Burke, the most insidious element of the French Revolution was its organized, ideological atheism: "a foul, unnatural vice, foe to all the dignity and consolation of mankind...." That suggestive description from the *Reflections* calls our attention to the fact that atheism was not a point of view but rather a "vice," and an "unnatural" one at that. The converse also held for Burke: Belief in what the *Regicide Peace* called "God as a moral governor of the world" was natural to man. Burke's own idea of Christianity was an innate faith that registered as feeling but was also reconcilable with reason. The established Anglican church, the *Reflections* explained, was "the first of our prejudices,—not a prejudice destitute of reason, but involving in it profound and extensive wisdom." That is, revelation elevated reason to the plane of wisdom.

We have seen Burke call religion the basis of civil society, but that does not mean he viewed it instrumentally. In his notebook from the 1750s, Burke observed that religion that did not command sincere faith could not be worthwhile to the state. "If you attempt to make the end of Religion to be its Utility to human Society, to make it only a sort of supplement to the Law, and insist principally on this Topic, as is very common to do," he wrote, "you then change its principle of Operation, which consists on Views beyond this Life," and thus make it worthless to civil society. In calling atheism a political evil and commending the political benefits of faith, Burke, in 1793 notes on the war with France, hoped not to be seen to think "religion nothing but policy...." He told his Irish friend William Smith in a 1795 letter that Smith should not apologize for his religious attachments: "Nothing is so fatal to Religion as indifference which is, at least, half Infidelity."

That did not mean religion was not valuable to civil society, only that it had to be believed sincerely to be useful. Burke endorsed established religion because it bound a political community together rather than leaving faith to the isolated individual conscience. "They who think religion of no importance to the state have abandoned it to the conscience or caprice of the individual; they make no provision for it whatsoever, but leave every club to make, or not, a voluntary contribution towards its support, according to their fancies," he wrote to Langrishe in 1792. He responded similarly to the Unitarian Society: "Religion is so far, in my opinion, from being out of the province or the duty of a Christian magistrate, that it is, and it ought to be, not only his care, but the principal thing in his care; because it is one of the great bonds of human society, and its object the supreme good, the ultimate end and object of man himself."

Jacobin atheism was for this reason, Burke noted in the 1793 notes, "the great *political* evil of the time" (emphasis added). In a 1795 letter to William Elliott, Burke described religion as the foundation of other social institutions. "Religion, that held the materials of the [social] fabric together, was first systematically loosened. All other opinions, under the name of prejudices, must fall along with it; and property, left undefended by principles, became a repository of spoils to tempt cupidity, and not a magazine to furnish arms for defence."

Atheism was also inherently expansionary because it was solely philosophical in nature and therefore transcended national boundaries. War
against France was therefore a defense of religion, but it is important
to note why religion was worth the fight: because it imparted "dignity"
and "hope" to human life. Burke argued in *Regicide Peace* that "if a war
to prevent Louis the Fourteenth from imposing his religion was just,
a war to prevent the murderers of Louis the Sixteenth from imposing
their irreligion upon us is just: a war to prevent the operation of a system
which makes life without dignity and death without hope is a just war."
The work continued: "Better this island should be sunk to the bottom of
the sea than that (so far as human infirmity admits) it should not be a
country of religion and morals!"

Religion was reasonable but, like political society, not subject to
limitless philosophical deconstruction. Religious beliefs, like political
society, were the products of prescription, or long use. He wrote in a 1795
letter advocating the emancipation of Irish Catholics: "All the principal
religions in Europe stand upon one common bottom. The support that
the whole or the favored parts may have in the secret dispensations of
Providence it is impossible to tell; but, humanly speaking, they are all *prescriptive* religions. They have all stood long enough to make prescription
and its chain of legitimate prejudices their main stay." Burke was generally
an advocate for toleration, but his Christian belief was deep. He told the
House of Lords in the Hastings trial:

> You have the representatives of that religion which says that their God
> is love, that the very vital spirit of their institution is charity,—a religion
> which so much hates oppression, that, when the God whom we adore
> appeared in human form, He did not appear in a form of greatness and
> majesty, but in sympathy with the lowest of the people, and thereby
> made it a firm and ruling principle that their welfare was the object of
> all government, since the Person who was the Master of Nature chose
> to appear Himself in a subordinate situation.

In fact, the Jacobins who set out to destroy religion were not only wrong,
the *Reflections* said. Their behavior was characteristic of "the selfish enlargement of mind and the narrow liberality of sentiment of insidious
men, which, commencing in close hypocrisy and fraud, have ended in

open violence and rapine." It is crucial to observe the difference between the flaws of reason and the flaws of feeling: Reason was deranged by being "enlarged," sentiment by being "narrowed."

With respect to reason, then, we can say Burke's prudence reflects a respect for ideas but an accommodation to circumstance, a greater confidence in feeling than abstraction, and a faith in revealed religion that could be reconciled with reason. Lincoln, too, felt a deep sense of belief. But his, and his mode of reasoning, differed fundamentally from Burke's. What they shared was a commitment to prudence. But the differences are unmistakable. In his "Speech on American Taxation," Burke said of the statesman William Pitt the Elder that "[f]or a wise man, he seemed to me [during the American crisis] to be governed too much by general maxims." Yet Lincoln, certainly a wise man, was so governed too.

ʂⱲ Ⱳ

Definitions and Axioms

Lincoln on Reason and Revelation

In an April 1859 letter responding to an invitation to attend a festival in Boston commemorating Jefferson's birthday, Lincoln paid heed to the drafter of the Declaration of Independence in terms that suggest a much more formal concept of reason than Burke's: "One would start with great confidence that he could convince any sane child that the simpler propositions of Euclid are true; but, nevertheless, he would fail, utterly, with one who should deny the definitions and axioms. The principles of Jefferson are the definitions and axioms of free society." The description of the Declaration's principles as "definitions and axioms" suggests Lincoln's method of reasoning from universal principles. In an 1859 speech in Columbus, Ohio, he similarly challenged his rival, Stephen A. Douglas, to demonstrate the defensibility of slavery "as Euclid demonstrated propositions." Lincoln knew of what he spoke: He reported in his 1860 campaign biography that he had taught himself "and nearly mastered the Six-books of Euclid."

Lincoln's idea of reason cannot be wholly reconciled with Burke's emphasis on circumstance and feeling, but it is entirely reconcilable with prudence. Lincoln did not, like Burke, write explicitly on the role of reason in politics, so we must generally derive his view of reason from how he employed the faculty. There are some references to reason, to be sure, mostly in his early rhetoric. Lincoln spoke often about the need to base political choices on reason rather than passion, as in the peroration of the Lyceum Address: Passion had supplied pillars for the Republic during the unique conditions of revolution, but no more.

> They *were* the pillars of the temple of liberty; and now, that they have crumbled away, that temple must fall, unless we, their descendants, supply their places with other pillars, hewn from the solid quarry of sober reason. Passion has helped us; but can do so no more. It will in future be our enemy. Reason, cold, calculating, unimpassioned reason, must furnish all the materials for our future support and defence.

It is difficult to imagine this reference to "cold, calculating, unimpassioned reason" emanating from Burke. Burke understood the danger of passions in politics but thought unbridled reason led inexorably to that risk. Nor was Burke likely to conclude something like the Temperance Address as Lincoln did, albeit in a formulation Harry V. Jaffa regards as ironic: "Happy day, when, all appetites controled, all passions subdued, all matters subjected, *mind*, all conquering *mind*, shall live and move the monarch of the world. Glorious consummation! Hail fall of Fury! Reign of Reason, all hail!" Burke's emphasis on feeling as a cementing and grounding principle likewise forms an instructive contrast with Lincoln's description of the issue of slavery in a March 1860 speech in New Haven, Connecticut: "Whenever this question shall be settled, it must be settled on some philosophical basis. No policy that does not rest upon some philosophical public opinion can be permanently maintained."

Still, we should take care before driving too broad a wedge between them. There is no question that Burke's method of separating metaphysical from political reasoning and, in the latter case, following an Aristotelian method of induction that reasoned upward from circumstances differs from Lincoln's more Platonic approach, which, as Jaffa persuasively observes, does focus on abstract principles. One suspects Burke would see some of Lincoln's early rhetoric about the power of reason as intemperate. On the other hand, Lincoln most famously applied this axiomatic method to the issue of slavery, which he confronted as a concrete wrong bound, as we have already seen in Chapter 2, by the limitations of circumstance. Humility suffused Lincoln's character, including in his application of reason, as in the letter he sent to the *Sangamo Journal* announcing his first campaign for state legislature. Lincoln noted that some had called for reform of a series of laws. He replied: "But considering the great probability that the framers of those laws were wiser than myself, I should prefer not meddling with them, unless they were first attacked by others, in which case I should feel it both a privilege and a duty to take that stand, which in my view, might tend most to the advancement of justice."

Moreover, Burke and Lincoln shared a suspicion of politics inflamed by passion. We have already encountered this suspicion in Burke, as in his opposition of "mean passions" to "heroic prudence" during parliamentary debate on America or his concern about the tendency of crowds to follow passion rather than logic. In a letter to his Springfield friend Andrew McCallen in June 1858, Lincoln likewise objected to the political tactic of inflaming issues by "noisy demonstrations—importing speakers from a distance and the like. They excite prejudice and close the avenues to sober reason." In 1857's celebrated *Rock Island Bridge Case*, in which he defended a bridge company against the owners of a steamboat that had crashed into it, Lincoln argued to the jury that the steamboat pilot could have employed his reason to assess the disputed height of a pier. "He should have discarded passion, and the chances are that he would have had no disaster at all."

In 1860's Cooper Union Address, Lincoln advised Republicans to *"do nothing through passion and ill temper. Even though the southern people will not so much as listen to us, let us calmly consider their demands, and yield to them if, in our deliberate view of our duty, we possibly can."* En route to Washington for his inauguration, he said at a flag-raising ceremony at Independence Hall that the tradition embodied in that place included "fraternal feeling" while "excluding passion, ill-temper and precipitate action on all occasions...." During the same journey, he predicted to the state legislature of New York that "if we have patience; if we restrain ourselves; if we allow ourselves not to run off in a passion," God would guide the country through the secession crisis. As president, Lincoln often commuted sentences if he felt an offender had been under the sway of, as he put it in one 1862 commutation, "sudden passion, and not of premeditation."

We have already seen that Lincoln felt consistent in advising Gen-

eral Joseph Hooker to display boldness but not "rashness." In an 1863
dispatch to General William S. Rosecrans, Lincoln felt it was necessary, in the course of imploring action, also to warn against rashness
not once, but twice: "I would not push you to any rashness; but I am
very anxious that you do your utmost, short of rashness" to contain
rebel General Braxton Bragg so he could not oppose Grant's pursuit
of Vicksburg.

Steven B. Smith argues that Lincoln blended the American tradition
of natural rights with an ethic of moral perfectionism associated with
Immanuel Kant. Smith does not deny Lincoln's prudence, but he does
suggest that Lincoln reasoned from universally applicable principles and
not merely from the authority of the past. There is much to commend this
account, especially insofar as Smith acknowledges that Lincoln moved
toward these universal principles prudently. Burke's position, by contrast,
was that applying such abstract principles in political life—especially
when they are derived from the rationalism of the individual moment
and not from custom accreted over time—inherently led to fanaticism
and even violence. For Lincoln, by contrast, a philosophical basis for argument anchored it by making it demonstrable to the faculty of reason
that everyone shared.

Lincoln's method lies somewhere between Burke's and Kant's.
There is no gainsaying Jaffa's understanding of Lincoln as reasoning
from abstract principles, but neither can it be denied that he sought
to employ these in correcting concrete wrongs, not attaining utopian
visions. There is a deep prudence in his criticism of Douglas in a July
1858 speech in Springfield: "He says this Dred Scott case is a very small
matter at most—that it has no practical effect; that at best, or rather, I
suppose, at worst, it is but an abstraction. I submit that the proposition
that the thing which determines whether a man is free or a slave is
rather *concrete* than abstract."

In this chapter, we shall engage several elements of Lincoln's concept
of reason: his reasoning from the internal logic of issues, but always with
a concrete end; his universalizing of his opponents' claims to show where
they led; and, finally, his belief that social progress would be driven by the
unleashing of innovative, intellectual energies. We shall then turn to his
oft-misunderstood view of religion.

Internal Logic

Perhaps the clearest and most compelling illustration of Lincoln's method of reasoning from universal principles to explicate the internal logic of an issue is his circa 1854 "Fragment on Slavery." It bears quotation in full:

> If A. can prove, however conclusively, that he may, of right, enslave B.—why may not B. snatch the same argument, and prove equally, that he may enslave A?—
>
> You say A. is white, and B. is black. It is *color*, then; the lighter, having the right to enslave the darker? Take care. By this rule, you are to be slave to the first man you meet, with a fairer skin than your own.
>
> You do not mean *color* exactly?—You mean the whites are *intellectually* the superiors of the blacks, and, therefore have the right to enslave them? Take care again. By this rule, you are to be slave to the first man you meet, with an intellect superior to your own.
>
> But, say you, it is a question of *interest*; and, if you can make it your *interest*, you have the right to enslave another. Very well. And if he can make it his interest, he has the right to enslave you.

This is a clear instance of exposing the logical heart of an issue without reference to any extrinsic empirical claim. Even the subjects and objects of the analysis are rendered as the generic variables "A" and "B." Lincoln dismantles the reasoning of Southern slavery apologists through what the Lyceum Address called "cold, calculating, unimpassioned reason." There is no appeal to pure emotion with regard to the cruelty of slavery, only a logical analysis of the issue. Its prudence lies in Lincoln's use of logic to appeal to the interest of the majority. The logic is grounded in a concrete issue that Lincoln practically confronts as a political actor. Lincoln also spurned pathos in arguing to the Wisconsin State Agricultural Society in 1859 that the wrongness of slavery was evident in the nature of humanity: Because "the Author of man makes every individual with one head and one pair of hands, it was probably intended that heads and hands should cooperate as friends; and that that particular head, should direct and control that particular pair of hands."

This reasoning descends directly from the classic mode of natural law. Lincoln's 1859 "Lecture on Discoveries and Inventions" also reasoned from observations about human nature. "[I]t would appear that speech was not an invention of man, but rather the direct gift of his Creator. But whether Divine gift, or invention, it is still plain that if a mode of communication had been left to invention, *speech* must have been the first, from the superior adaption to the end, of the organs of speech, over every other means within the whole range of nature." One reason was that "[t]he inclination to exchange thoughts with one another is probably an original impulse of our nature."

The Peoria Address proceeded by a similar method, cutting to the essence of the slavery dispute: whether African Americans were human beings: "Equal justice to the south, it is said, requires us to consent to the extending of slavery to new countries. That is to say, inasmuch as you do not object to my taking my hog to Nebraska, therefore I must not object to you taking your slave. Now, I admit this is perfectly logical, if there is no difference between hogs and negroes." Yet, again operating in the realm of circumstance, Lincoln noted that Southerners themselves, who were actuated by "human sympathies" no less than Northerners, did not act on the extreme consequences of their own proposition. Many had freed their slaves, often at great expense, thus betraying a latent knowledge that they were human. This "moral sense" argument is an integral part of Lincoln's argument for natural justice, and he made it by analogy. There were more than 433,000 free African Americans in the country, he noted: "We do not see free horses or free cattle running at large. How is this? All these free blacks are the descendants of slaves, or have been slaves themselves, and they would be slaves now, but for SOMETHING which has operated on their white owners, inducing them, at vast pecuniary sacrifices, to liberate them."

In the 1858 "House Divided" address, Lincoln inferred from the nature of slavery itself that it had to expand or perish. Such was the universalizing logic of Douglas's doctrine of "popular sovereignty." "In *my* opinion, [the slavery controversy] *will* not cease, until a *crisis* shall have been reached, and passed…. Either the *opponents* of slavery, will arrest the further spread of it, and place it where the public mind shall rest in the belief that it is in course of ultimate extinction, or its *advocates* will push it forward, till it shall become alike lawful in all the States…." This, again, was rooted in his audience's interest: If the free states permitted the expansion of slavery, it would eventually spread into their own territory. There would be no end, he said in the Lincoln-Douglas debates, even to the point of imperial expansionism. "If Judge Douglas's policy upon this question succeeds, and gets fairly settled down, until all opposition is crushed out, the next thing will be a grab for the territory of poor Mexico, an invasion of the rich lands of South America, then the adjoining islands will follow, each one of which promises additional slave fields." This was an example of a method of reasoning Lincoln often employed: the *reductio ad absurdum*.

The Reductio ad Absurdum

A comparable method of reasoning from the intrinsic nature of an issue was evident in Lincoln's 1839 speech on the "Sub-Treasury," a proposal to place government funds in independent depositories—what Lincoln satirized as "iron boxes"—rather than banks. Like Chief Justice John Marshall's opinion in *McCulloch v. Maryland*, which established the constitutionality of a national bank, Lincoln reasoned from the internal logic of the Constitution's "necessary and proper" clause, which allows Congress to do what is "necessary and proper" to execute its explicitly enumerated powers. Lincoln noted the logical absurdity of critics who said government had to demonstrate "indispensable necessity" for measures enacted under this clause. Such reasoning would "exclude every sort of fiscal agent that the mind of man can conceive. A [National] *Bank* is not *indispensable*, because we can take the *Sub-Treasury*; the *Sub-Treasury* is not indispensable because we can take the *Bank*. The rule is too absurd to need further comment." The argument, which Lincoln employed frequently, is a *reductio ad absurdum*: demonstrating the falseness of a proposition on the grounds that it leads to absurd results.

He used the same device in a congressional debate on internal improvements in June 1848. Opponents said such improvements to roads, canals, railroads, and other channels of commerce would disproportionately benefit the localities in which they were made. The results of carrying that argument to its conclusion would be anarchic, since if the national government must refuse local benefits on this ground, states could decline participation in national investments because their benefits were too general. Lincoln explained the universalizing logic:

"Thus it is seen, that if this argument of 'inequality' is sufficient any where,—it is sufficient every where; and puts an end to improvements altogether." Lincoln wryly likened the inequality argument to abolishing the presidency because its costs were general while its benefits were personal: "An honest laborer digs coal at about seventy cents a day, while the president digs abstractions at about seventy dollars a day. The *coal* is clearly worth more than the *abstractions*, and yet what a monstrous inequality in the prices! Does the president, for this reason, propose to abolish the presidency?"

Lincoln most shone in this method of reasoning in the slavery controversy. At Peoria, he explained that the same logic that said each state could decide the issue of slavery for itself also dictated that each individual could decide for himself, a prospect that would nationalize slavery. "What better moral right have thirty-one citizens of Nebraska to say, that the thirty-second shall not hold slaves, than the people of the thirty-one states have to say that slavery shall not go into the thirty-second State at all?" He proceeded to show the absurd consequences of applying that principle: The international slave trade could not be banned because he who has a "sacred right" to own slaves in Nebraska also had an equally "sacred right" to purchase them, which would doubtless occur on the African coast. This was true, he added with his trademark dry humor, "provided you will consent to not hang them for going there to buy them," a penalty the law of the time provided for international slave traders.

Again, notice the combination of the abstract and the concrete: The *reductio* in these cases is directed toward showing the people that their own laws would become absurd under Douglas's warped understanding of "self-government." Lincoln thus said in the first Lincoln-Douglas debate, held at Ottawa, Illinois, that Douglas's proclaimed agnosticism on the question of slavery would "penetrat[e] the human soul and eradicat[e] the light of reason and the love of liberty in this American people." The reasoning faculty, in other words, was inseparable from the soul. He argued at New Haven that apologists for slavery could not contain the logic of "self-government," which would eventually force slavery on the free states. "Demanding what they do, and for the reason they do, they can voluntarily stop nowhere short of this consummation. Holding, as they do, that Slavery is morally right, and socially elevating, they cannot cease to demand a full national recognition of it, as a legal right, and a social blessing. Nor can we justifiably withhold this, on any ground save our conviction that Slavery is wrong."

The same method of universalizing a principle to show its consequences is evident in Lincoln's 1857 speech on *Dred Scott*, the Supreme Court decision that had denied the full humanity of African Americans and overturned the Missouri Compromise. Lincoln's target was not simply the decision itself, but also Douglas's claim that the Supreme Court deserved absolute acquiescence. We can watch Lincoln proceed with care from the principle to its universal consequences: "Now, if this is sound, as to this particular constitutional question, it is equally sound of *all* constitutional questions; so that the proposition substantially, is 'Whatever decision the Supreme court makes on *any* constitutional question, must be obeyed, and enforced by all the departments of the federal government.'"

The First Inaugural deployed the *reductio* to show the illogic of secession: "If a minority, in such case [of disagreement with the majority], will secede rather than acquiesce, they make a precedent which, in turn, will divide and ruin them; for a minority of their own will secede from them, whenever a majority refuses to be controlled by such minority.... Plainly, the central idea of secession, is the essence of anarchy." Again, Lincoln grounded this rational appeal in the interest of his audience. Likewise, in his message to the Congress he called into special session at the onset of the war, Lincoln said the secessionists had "invented an ingenious sophism which, if conceded, was followed by perfectly logical steps, through all the incidents, to the complete destruction of the Union."

As Smith notes, Lincoln's reasoning method included a cosmopolitan element, though it must be emphasized that Lincoln meant America had a duty to demonstrate the decency of self-government, not to undertake missionary work to spread it. In the message to Congress we have just encountered, Lincoln said the controversy "embraces more than the fate of these United States. It presents to the whole family of man, the question, whether a constitutional republic, or a democracy—a government of the people, by the same people—can, or cannot, maintain its territorial integrity, against its own domestic foes." The success of secession ideology would "practically put an end to free government upon the earth."

At Edwardsville, Illinois, during the 1858 U.S. Senate campaign, Lincoln denied that "the bulwark of our own liberty and independence" lay in military might, which could as easily be turned against liberty as protect it. We can see once more that his universalism was prudently grounded in an appeal to concrete interest:

> Our reliance is in the *love of liberty* which God has planted in our bosoms. Our defense is in the preservation of the spirit which prizes liberty as the heritage of all men, in all lands, every where. Destroy this spirit, and you have planted the seeds of despotism around your own doors. Familiarize yourselves with the chains of bondage, and you are preparing your own limbs to wear them. Accustomed to trample on the rights of those around you, you have lost the genius of your own independence, and become the fit subjects of the first cunning tyrant who rises.

Moreover, in a compatibility with Burke that is vital to understanding Lincoln's reason, principle did not mandate positive political action. As we have seen, he said at Cincinnati in 1859 that slavery was an absolute wrong and that yielding to any encouragement of it was yielding to the institution itself. However, "[w]hen I say this, I do not mean to say that this general government is charged with the duty of redressing or preventing all the wrongs in the world; but I do think that it is charged with the duty of preventing and redressing all wrongs which are wrongs to itself."

Lincoln's reasoning method was by no means what Burke called "metaphysical mad[ness]." Lincoln was undoubtedly more devoted to "general maxims" than Burke would counsel, but Lincoln's general maxims invariably applied to concrete circumstances. Moreover, unlike the French Declaration of the Rights of Man and Citizen, Lincoln's maxims were essentially reactive, a Burkean form of reforming in order to restore. That is, his maxims were used to correct—to restore the ideals of the Declaration of Independence—not to create. This served a prudential grounding function that was reflected in Lincoln's lifelong moderation on the issue even as he pursued ultimate objects. Burke's concern, by contrast, was a universalizing reason unmoored to practical political life, not again, because he was unreasonable but because he was eminently so—enough to recognize reason's limits. Lincoln's writings, from his first letter to the people of Sangamo County to the Second Inaugural, were likewise suffused with humility.

Reason and Progress

The intellectual faculty was also an agent of progress, rendered here deliberately in the lowercase. Put otherwise, he assumed human knowledge and prosperity were capable of sustained growth fueled by reason, but he never spoke of either the moral perfectibility of man or an inherent tendency of history to move in the direction of enlightenment. This was most evident in the "Lecture on Discoveries and Inventions" in 1859, in which Lincoln drew a metaphor distinguishing between "Young America," animated by innovation, and "Old Fogy," the element that resisted progress. "Young America" had a "horror [of] all that is old…and if there be anything which he can endure, it is only old whiskey and old tobacco."

Yet Lincoln was sympathetic to Old Fogy. Early man was necessarily ignorant of such matters as technology in comparison to contemporary generations, yet he warned against "the Youngster discard[ing] all he has learned from others," in which case the advantage of youth would disappear. "The great difference between Young America and Old Fogy, is the result of *Discoveries, Inventions,* and *Improvements. These*, in turn, are the result of *observation, reflection* and *experiment*": that is, reason. Adam, the original Old Fogy, had no means of discovery, a concept that itself had to be invented. Hence Lincoln's reflections on speech, which we encountered earlier. Some inventions, especially writing and printing, particularly propelled progress.

The free labor platform of the Republican Party was also directed toward improvement. He explained in Cincinnati in 1859 that a common laborer had the capacity by thrift and industry to improve his condition: "This progress by which the poor, honest, industrious, and resolute man raises himself, that he may work on his own account, and hire somebody else, is that progress that human nature is entitled to, is that improvement in condition that is intended to be secured by those institutions under which we live, is the great principle for which this government was really formed." Note again that the progress pertains to man's "condition"—that is, his material existence—and not to his nature. Human nature was a constant. Lincoln had said in the Temperance Address that hounding alcoholics into abstinence "was to expect a reversal of human nature, which is God's decree, and can never be reversed."

The nation's pursuit of equality, too, was a matter of progress, but in this case progress toward an ancient ideal, not new discoveries. In an 1858 speech at Lewistown, Illinois, Lincoln revered the Declaration as an ideal the founding generation knew they could not themselves attain: "They grasped not only the whole race of man then living, but they reached forward and seized upon the farthest posterity. They erected a beacon to guide their children and their children's children, and the countless myriads who should inhabit the earth in other ages." The Constitution's approach was similar: He noted at Peoria that the Constitution concealed its references to slavery in such phrases as "person held to service or labor": "Thus, the thing is hid away, in the constitution, just as an afflicted man hides away a wen or cancer, which he dares not cut out at once, lest he bleed to death; with the promise, nevertheless, that the cutting may begin at the end of a given time." In his frequent comparisons of slavery to cancer, the metaphor, as Lewis Lehrman has observed, "was to cut the cancer slowly so as to save the patient." This was prudent progress: to be achieved over the long run without damaging its own object by rushing.

Lincoln's Faith

In October 1863, Lincoln prepared two versions of remarks to the Baltimore Presbyterian Synod. In the first, though not the second, he remarked: "I have often wished that I was a more devout man than I am." His meaning is obscure. It could have been a statement of humility, refusing to claim for himself the mantle of faith, or it could just as likely have meant Lincoln was not devout. But two points are salient. One is that Lincoln's writings from his earliest days to his final speeches are shot through with Biblical references—from the "house divided" to, replying to a speech by the mayor of Philadelphia when he was en route to his inauguration, saying "may my right hand forget its cunning and my tongue cleave to the roof of my mouth, if I ever prove false to [the teachings of the Declaration]"—and his meditations on divinity grew as the crisis of the Civil War mounted. The second is that he "wished" he was "more" devout, which is to say he felt some devotion and, significantly, wished to feel more. The presence of this devotion was evident the next month in the Gettysburg Address, in which Lincoln appeared extemporaneously to have added the qualification "under God" to the phrase "this nation."

Several commentators, including David Lowenthal and Richard Brookhiser, have concluded that Lincoln may have been an atheist. Some of Lincoln's contemporaries suspected the same. In his 1846 campaign for Congress, he was compelled to deny being a "scoffer at religion." He suggested he had repudiated his early belief in the Doctrine of Necessity, the belief that undermined free will by holding, as Lincoln put it, "that the human mind is impelled to action, or held in rest by some power, over which the mind itself has no control...." Lincoln said he could not support an "open enemy" of religion, if only because such cynicism would "insult the feelings, and injure the morals, of the community in which he may live."

But Lincoln was remarkably reflective about divinity—never in sectarian or orthodox terms, to be sure, but not in areligious ones either— especially but not exclusively during the war. We have already encountered his references to God and the Creation in the context of slavery. He employed these repeatedly, as in the 1858 speech at Lewistown: The Declaration reflected the founders' "enlightened belief, nothing stamped with the Divine image and likeness was sent into the world to be trodden on, and degraded, and imbruted by its fellows." As president, Lincoln received a petition from the historian and diplomat George Bancroft in November 1861 asserting that "Civil war is the instrument of Divine Providence to root out social slavery...." Lincoln responded sympathetically but prudently: That "main thought...is one which does not escape my attention, and with which I must deal in all caution, and with the best judgment I can bring to it." The next year, he responded to a delegation of Evangelical Lutherans in tones that linked Divinity with progress: "[I]f it shall please the Divine Being who determines the destinies of nations that this shall remain a united people, they will, humbly seeking the Divine guidance, make their prolonged national existence a source of new benefits to themselves and their successors, and to all classes and conditions of mankind."

Lincoln issued several proclamations of national fast days that were striking for their suggestion that sin and faithlessness caused the bloodshed. In 1861, for instance, he complied with a congressional request that he proclaim a national fast day. The proclamation was frank

in its acknowledgment of human frailty and divine superintendence
of the war:

> And whereas it is fit and becoming in all people, at all times, to acknowl-
> edge and revere the Supreme Government of God; to bow in humble
> submission to his chastisements; to confess and deplore their sins and
> transgressions in the full conviction that the fear of the Lord is the be-
> ginning of wisdom; and to pray, with all fervency and contrition, for the
> pardon of their past offences, and for a blessing upon their present and
> prospective action....

A March 1863 proclamation, issued at the behest of a Senate with which
he "fully concurred," went even further. The nation had prospered since
its founding. "But we have forgotten God.... Intoxicated with unbroken
success, we have become too self-sufficient to feel the necessity of re-
deeming and preserving grace, too proud to pray to the God that made
us! It behooves us then, to humble ourselves before the offended Power,
to confess our national sins, and to pray for clemency and forgiveness."

After major Union victories, it was often Lincoln's custom to proclaim
days of thanksgiving, as he did just after Gettysburg in July 1863 in his
characteristically encouraging rather than anathematic tones: "I invite the
People of the United States to assemble on that occasion in their customary places of worship, and in the forms approved by their own consciences,
render the homage due to the Divine Majesty, for the wonderful things
he has done in the Nation's behalf...." Following the capture of Atlanta,
he called for "devout acknowledgement to the Supreme Being in whose
hands are the destinies of nations."

There is a sense of remove in some of these references to "the Supreme
Being" or the "Divine Majesty." But while Lincoln was never an orthodox
Christian, he plainly felt a deep and, crucially, personal faith that deep-
ened with crisis. In his farewell address to the people of Springfield in
February 1861, as he departed for his inauguration as president, he noted
the gravity of the secession crisis. "Without the assistance of that Divine
Being, who ever attended him, I cannot succeed. With that assistance I
cannot fail." Along the journey to Washington, he told the New Jersey
Senate that "I shall be most happy indeed if I shall be an humble instrument in the hands of the Almighty, and of this, his almost chosen people,

for perpetuating the object of that great struggle," by which he meant the American Revolution's devotion to natural equality.

This notion of being a "humble instrument" fermented in Lincoln through the war. He wrote to Albert Hodges in April 1864 that his belief in the policies of his administration was "no compliment to my own sagacity": "I claim not to have controlled events, but confess plainly that events have controlled me. Now, at the end of three years struggle the nation's condition is not what either party, or any man devised, or expected. God alone can claim it. Whither it is tending seems plain. If God now wills the removal of a great wrong, and wills also that we of the North as well as you of the South, shall pay fairly for our complicity in that wrong, impartial history will find therein new cause to attest and revere the justice and goodness of God." Observe the grounding in circumstance implicit in the notion of being controlled by events. This separates Lincoln's greatness from our contemporary quest for presidential legacies, which fuels change for change's sake in direct contravention of the Lyceum Address.

Similarly, in an 1862 "Meditation on the Divine Will," Lincoln wrote that God's purpose in the Civil War might not be that of either North or South: "I am almost ready to say this is probably true—that God wills this contest, and wills that it shall not end yet. By his mere quiet power, on the minds of the now contestants, He could have either *saved* or *destroyed* the Union without a human contest. Yet the contest began. And having begun He could give the final victory to either side any day. Yet the contest proceeds." These Divine purposes were not always comprehensible. He wrote in September 1864 to Eliza Gurney, the head of a visiting delegation of Quakers, that Americans had hoped the "[t]he purposes of the Almighty are perfect, and must prevail, though we erring mortals may fail to accurately perceive them in advance."

"Erring mortals" is an important formulation. History easily enough demonstrates that feeling like an instrument of God can make leaders into zealots. But Lincoln's theology was eminently prudent. First, he used it as often to chasten as to inspire, as we have seen in the fast-day proclamations. Second, Lincoln, like Burke, felt religion was reconcilable with reason, which provided it with prudential grounding. Campaigning for the Whig ticket in Worcester, Massachusetts, in 1848, Lincoln was the essence of classical prudence: He denied both the Free Soil claim that

Whigs were pro-slavery and the abolitionist argument that men should
"do their duty and leave the consequences to God." The latter "merely
gave an excuse for taking a course that they were not able to maintain
by a fair and full argument. To make this declaration did not show what
their duty was. If it did we should have no use for judgment, we might
as well be made without intellect...."

Speaking at Cincinnati in September 1859, Lincoln declared: "I hold
that if there is any one thing that can be proved to be the will of God
by external nature around us, without reference to revelation, it is the
proposition that whatever any one man earns with his hands and by the
sweat of his brow, he shall enjoy in peace." In Hartford in 1860, Lincoln
repeated this Thomist analysis of slavery: "I think that if anything can
be proved by natural theology, it is that slavery is morally wrong. God
gave man a mouth to receive bread, hands to feed it, and his hand as a
right to carry bread to his mouth without controversy." The key word in
both instances is "proved." Faith was accessible to reason, and the particular conclusion that slavery was wrong did not require revelation. But
prudence was necessary in the application of reason in such matters. In
a private note written around 1858, Lincoln observed that "[t]he sum of
pro-slavery theology seems to be this: 'Slavery is not universally *right*,
nor yet universally *wrong*; it is better for *some* people to be slaves; and,
in such cases, it is the Will of God that they be such.' Certainly there is
no contending against the Will of God; but still there is some difficulty
in ascertaining, and applying it, to particular cases." This is precisely the
kind of prudence that Aquinas said imparted human freedom: a Divine
end with prudential choice of means for attaining it.

Lincoln's prudent theology reached its apotheosis in his Second
Inaugural. There, Lincoln acknowledged a unity of North and South
under the same God, to Whom both sides prayed, even as he delivered
the damning indictment: "It may seem strange that any men should dare
to ask a just God's assistance in wringing their bread from the sweat of
other men's faces; but"—immediately soothing the severity of Genesis
with the mildness of Matthew—"let us judge not that we be not judged."
Twice the Biblical imagery subtly shifts. In Genesis, as Steven B. Smith
has noted, to eat by the sweat of one's own brow is a punishment; here it
is a privilege. The emphasis is on "other": the sin is to wring one's bread
from the sweat of *other* men's faces. In Matthew, as Smith has also em-

phasized, the passage "judge not" is an admonition: Judge not that *you* be not judged. Lincoln, having of course delivered a devastating judgment, moderates the Gospel to the gentler assumption of shared responsibility implicit in first person plural: Judge not that *we* be not judged.

In the spirit of the Temperance Address, Lincoln expresses himself morally without moralizing, noting that the prayer of neither side has been "answered fully." Then the key: The hard edge of reason in earlier addresses has given way to a prudent respect for what sounds very much like Divine grace. "The Almighty has His own purposes. 'Woe unto the world because of offences! for it must needs be that offences come; but woe to that man by whom the offence cometh!'" Again the reference is to the Gospel of Matthew. This is neither determinism, it bears emphasis, nor philosophical necessity. Man is responsible for his actions even as he is an instrument of God. The offense was going to happen; the sinner did not have to choose to be its particular causal agent. Indeed, Lincoln immediately casts the war as the due punishment of North *and* South: the South for its embrace of slavery, the North not just for its tolerance of but also for its interlocking gains from the evil institution.

We hope and pray, Lincoln notes, for a quick end to the conflict. "Yet," in perhaps the most rhetorically gifted turn of the address, a sentence that could not be diminished or distended by a single word, "if God wills that it continue, until all the wealth piled by the two hundred and fifty years of unrequited toil shall be sunk, and until every drop of blood drawn with the lash, shall be paid by another drawn with the sword, as was said three thousand years ago, so still it must be said, 'the judgments of the Lord, are true and righteous altogether.'"

The reference is to Psalm 19. The full verse refers not just to the righteousness of the Lord but also to "the fear of the Lord." And indeed this is a fearful expression of principle, for God exacts retribution for its violation. As Reinhold Niebuhr teaches in his magisterial reading of the Second Inaugural, we see imperfectly yet must judge as best we can. Lincoln's faith does not justify quietism. It does not reflect determinism. Rather, it guides resolve.

This limited knowledge yet determination to work within it defines the justly famous closing sequence of the Second Inaugural, which once more mitigates severity with warmth: "With malice toward none; with charity for all; with firmness in the right, as God gives us to see the

right, let us strive on to finish the work we are in...." Lincoln claims no
crystalline clarity of perception as to the right: We see it "as God gives
us" to see it—in other words "to the extent" God allows us to see it. This
humility is part of the essence of prudence, for Lincoln's modesty does
not imply vacillation. To the extent that we see the right, we are firm in
it. This is principle. Prudence governs it by acknowledging the limits of
what we are permitted to see.

We have already seen that Lincoln wrote to Thurlow Weed roughly
a week after the Second Inaugural that he accepted the "humiliation"
implicit in the address. By "humiliation" Lincoln meant neither shame
nor embarrassment. He referred the imposition or acceptance of humility.
Here reason and grace converge, for reason rightly understood—prudent
reason—recognizes reason's limits.

The Second Inaugural thus tells us that prudence must superintend
principle and mediate between accommodation and ideals. There is no
mechanistic formula to guide us. Identifying which issues are ultimate
requires a faculty of judgment, as does identifying when to press them.
It bears emphasis as well that by the time of the Second Inaugural, the
"cold, calculating, unimpassioned reason" of the Lyceum Address has
given way to grace and a humble deference to God's justice and will. This
reflects a mature humility that lies at the heart of prudence for Lincoln
as for Burke, yet Lincoln's embrace of human agency and responsibility
indicates an enduring understanding of the centrality of judgment.

CHAPTER FIVE

ഔ ൦ള

The Little Catechism of the Rights of Man

Burke on Liberty

Burke's February 1790 "Speech on the Army Estimates" marked the first time he addressed Parliament on his views on the French Revolution. Prefiguring the fracture in the Whig Party that was to come, he denounced the philosophical basis of the event with which his partisan colleagues had grown enchanted. The French, Burke declared, "made and recorded a sort of *institute* and digest of anarchy, called the Rights of Man, in such a pedantic abuse of elementary principles as would have disgraced boys at school...." This turned many of his Whig colleagues' heads. Burke had, after all, invoked "the natural rights of mankind" in the debate over Charles James Fox's East India Bill just over six years before, and, as we shall see, variations on this theme dot his rhetoric not just on India but on America, Ireland, and other topics as well. The debate persists in Burke scholarship to this day. For Mansfield, "[i]f there is one recurrent theme in Burke's letters, speeches, and writings, it is his emphasis on the moral and political evils that follow upon the intrusion of theory into political practice." Yet Peter J. Stanlis, Russell Kirk, and Francis Canavan, among others, emphasize the importance of the natural law, a theoretical grounding, to Burke's thought.

There is a consistent, navigable course through this terrain. Burke does endorse universal natural rights, but they are moral rights and they are the most basic of human entitlements: rights against murder, rapine, and slavery, for example. As Joseph Pappin III has noted, Burkean rights are concrete rather than abstract: They are, in Pappin's words, "those actual, concrete liberties and benefits which have been secured over time, reflect the traditions of a nation and are recognized and expressed in charters and covenants that give them a status and respect which makes them practically inalienable save for just cause. Time, history and tradition provide an important sanction and safeguard for these rights...."

The defining feature of politics, as opposed to morals, is variability according to circumstance. Burke's natural rights, then, are not rights to political arrangements, which he regards as artificial and therefore regulable. He wrote in the *Reflections*: "The moment you abate anything from the full rights of men each to govern himself, and suffer any artificial, positive limitation upon those rights, from that moment the whole organization of government becomes a consideration of convenience." Mansfield is correct: Theory cannot intrude into *political* practice. It remains very much relevant to moral understanding. "There are some fundamental points in which Nature never changes; but they are few and obvious, and belong rather to morals than to politics," Burke wrote in a speech he began drafting in 1793 on allied policy toward France. "But so far as regards political matter, the human mind and human affairs are susceptible of infinite modifications, and of combinations wholly new and unlooked-for."

With this in mind, we can understand the full passage alluded to above in the Speech on the Army Estimates. Having called the doctrine of the Rights of Man "pedantic," he continued:

> [B]ut this declaration of rights was worse than trifling and pedantic in them; as by their name and authority they systematically destroyed every hold of authority by opinion, religious or civil, on the minds of the people. By this mad declaration they subverted the state, and brought on such calamities as no country, without a long war, has ever been known to suffer, and which may in the end produce such a war, and perhaps many such.

The natural rights of mankind that Burke defended in America, India, and Ireland were constructive—"cementing principles," as he had described moderation in the letter to Depont—whereas the Rights of Man sought to destroy social ties. Crucially, these rights were to positive political arrangements. Moreover, the French doctrine was rooted in an aggressive atheism and leveling of property that actively undermined institutions essential to civil life.

We shall see in this chapter that the Americans, Irish, and Indians were deprived of legitimate rights whose restoration entailed no political upheaval or inconvenience. The French doctrine of the Rights of Man, by contrast, sought to entitle all people in all circumstances to positive political practices of the sort that Burke thought could only be formed according to local convenience. They were, as he derided them, "abstract rights" disconnected from the realities of political life. "What is the use of discussing a man's abstract right to food or medicine?" he inquired in the *Reflections*. "The question is upon the method of procuring and administering them. In that deliberation I shall always advise to call in the aid of the farmer and the physician, rather than the professor of metaphysics." The professor of metaphysics was not merely a useless participant in political life but also a positively dangerous one. Metaphysical politics was by its nature universal and therefore expansionist. It recognized neither borders, customs, nor the particularity of political life. It sought to bend human beings to theories rather than accommodate theories to human nature. It was therefore both destructive and dangerous, whereas genuine rights sought to foster connection and stability.

"The Pretended Rights of Men"

This dependable and therefore prudential basis for genuine rights was opposed to what Burke often qualified with such modifiers as the "pretended" rights of man. As we have already seen, genuine rights were placed on the sure basis of inheritance, whereas theoretical principle was a flimsy foundation on which they could be blown about. Thus the *Reflections*, describing Burke's British constitutional forebears: "[F]or reasons worthy of that practical wisdom which superseded their theoretic science, they preferred this positive, recorded, *hereditary* title to all which can be dear to man and the citizen to that vague, speculative right which exposed their sure inheritance to be scrambled for and torn to pieces by every wild, litigious spirit." This is a clear allusion to the French Declaration of the Rights of Man and the Citizen. Its rights were unstable by virtue of being speculative rather than customary, because while custom evolved only gradually, it was only too easy for another speculation to come along. Speculation itself invited it.

Because these French rights were theoretical, they purported to speak to all men at all times and thus knew no respect for borders or for the particularity of political communities. They were inherently aggressive. In 1793, Burke wrote to the Comte de Mercy that "[w]e are at war with a principle, and an example, which there is no shutting out by Fortresses or excluding by Territorial Limits. No lines of demarcation can bound the Jacobin Empire." Henry the Eighth, whom Burke described as a tyrant, was only a limited one because, the *Reflections* explained, he "had not studied in [the French] new schools [and] did not know what an effectual instrument of despotism was to be found in that grand magazine of offensive weapons, the rights of men." Instead, when Henry sought to "rob the abbeys" as the Jacobins had plundered the churches, he felt compelled first to accuse them of crimes. "Had fate reserved him to our times, four technical terms would have done his business, and saved him all this trouble; he needed nothing more than one short form of incantation:—'Philosophy, Light, Liberality, the Rights of Men.'"

Burke's reference to an "incantation" reminds us of the religious zeal of this decidedly secular revolution—in *Thoughts on French Affairs*, he described the rights of man as a "little catechism"—and it is worth asking why exactly these terms provided such a "grand magazine of offensive weapons." To oppose "philosophy" and "light" is to be irrational, less than fully human. To oppose "liberality" and "the rights of men" is to reject one's brothers. Either makes one disposable, if not outright culpable. For this reason, the *Reflections* continued, any sin of the Revolution was excused by "the 'all-atoning name' of Liberty." The Rights of Men could only operate in extremes and thus could not tolerate custom. The *Reflections* explained:

> They despise experience as the wisdom of unlettered men; and as for the
> rest, they have wrought under ground a mine that will blow up, at one

grand explosion, all examples of antiquity, all precedents, charters, and acts of Parliament. They have "the rights of men." Against these there can be no prescription; against these no argument is binding: these admit no temperament and no compromise: anything withheld from their full demand is so much of fraud and injustice. Against these their rights of men let no government look for security in the length of its continuance, or in the justice and lenity of its administration.

We shall see in considering Burke's understanding of genuine rights in the next section that this prescription, whether pertaining to ownership of property or a common stake in political tradition, was compatible with theory but refracted through practice. The French doctrine of human rights was grounded solely in contemporaneous notions of the rational and consequently had no place for "the collected reason of ages." By its nature, it had to be hostile to anything that did not conform to theoretical ideals, which is to say anything that existed at all. In turn, these theoretical ideals stoked the imagination with romantic hopes of what could be; hence Jacobin zeal.

Burke particularly worried that Jacobin zeal would take the place of Roman Catholicism in Ireland if the people's native religion was harassed out of existence or forced underground. In 1795, he wrote to William Smith that Burke's entire politics in the twilight of his life "center[ed] in one point; and to this the merit or demerit of every measure, (with me) is referable,—that is, what will most promote or depress the cause of Jacobinism." The persecution of Catholics, especially the suppression of their educational institutions, served this cause. "Let them grow lax, skeptical, careless and indifferent with regard to religion, and, so sure as we have an existence, it is not a zealous Anglican or Scottish Church principle, but direct Jacobinism, which will enter that breach." The choice, therefore, was not between Catholicism and some other form of Christianity, but rather between full toleration for Catholics and atheistic Jacobinism. He had similarly written to his son Richard in 1793: "It is the new fanatical religion, now in the heat of its first ferment, of the Rights of Man, which rejects all establishments, all discipline, all ecclesiastical, and in truth all civil order, which will triumph, and which will lay prostrate your church, which will destroy your distinctions, and which will put all your properties to auction, and disperse you over the earth."

The essence of Jacobinism was annihilation: the leveling of property, the undermining of religious faith and, above all, the destruction
of mutual commitment. The Revolution was intoxicated with novelty.
This was why, Burke wrote in *Thoughts on French Affairs*, the marauding
French "[made] it always their business, and often their public profession, to destroy all traces of ancient establishments, and to form a new
commonwealth in each country [they conquered], upon the basis of
the French *Rights of Man*." In the *Appeal*, Burke noted the tendency of
Jacobinism toward the erasure of any sense of obligation to the past or to
one another. "The pretended *rights of man*, which have made this havoc,
cannot be the rights of the people. For to be a people, and to have these
rights, are things incompatible. The one supposes the presence, the other
the absence, of a state of civil society." The very definition of civil life, the
life of citizens, lay in obligation. One reason, Burke wrote in *Regicide
Peace*, was the inexorable interdependence of people on one another. "As
to the right of men to act anywhere according to their pleasure, without
any moral tie, no such right exists. Men are never in a state of *total* independence of each other." This political or civil nature of rights was why,
as we have seen, their boundaries could not be defined with axiomatic
precision. Burke's denial of total independence also entailed a critique of
social contract theorizing, which assumed precisely such independence
and a rejection of man's natural sociality.

It was a common mistake to confuse, Burke wrote, principles of law,
which were exact, with those of politics, which were not. The *Appeal*
characterized the argument of the *Reflections* in these terms: "The foundation of government is there laid, not in imaginary rights of men, (which
at best is a confusion of judicial with civil principles,) but in political
convenience, and in human nature,—either as that nature is universal,
or as it is modified by local habits and social aptitudes." Political matters
could not be settled with arithmetic precision. They occupied the realm
of prudence. In 1792, writing to Langrishe, Burke had made a similar
distinction with respect to the voting rights of Irish Catholics. "[T]he
whole question comes before Parliament as a matter for its prudence.
I do not put the thing on a question of right. That discretion, which in
judicature is well said by Lord Coke to be a crooked cord, in legislature
is a golden rule." The reason was not that Burke was hostile to rights, but
rather that he sufficiently valued them to wish them to be balanced and
cemented by prudence.

Prudence was applied to what Burke characterized as "art," or, in more contemporary parlance, "artifice" or "convention": man's generational improvement of his natural condition. Artifice separated the pristine rights of a supposed natural paradise from the civil rights of a real political condition. "[A]s to the share of power, authority, and direction which each individual ought to have in the management of the state," Burke wrote in the *Reflections*, "that I must deny to be amongst the direct original rights of man in civil society; for I have in my contemplation the civil social man, and no other. It is a thing to be settled by convention." As we shall presently see, convention was not a license for anything, but it did preclude wild speculation. This endorsement of convention was also Burke's rejection of antinomianism—the view that denied the legitimacy of law because it was law—in all its forms.

The attempt to instantiate a pristine image of nature was not only impossible but perilous. Burke had written to Depont in 1789 that a "defect" in the state could actually be a "corrective" and that, in any event, such a defect could be tolerable and removable. "In that case, Prudence (in all things a Virtue, in Politicks the first of Virtues) will lead us rather to acquiesce in some qualified plan that does not come up to the full perfection of the abstract Idea, than to push for the more perfect, which cannot be attain'd without tearing to pieces the whole contexture of the commonwealth, and creating an heart-ache in a thousand worthy bosoms. In that case combining the means and end, the less perfect is the more desirable." The *Reflections* develops this formulation—that the imperfect is not only tolerable but positively better because it is adapted to the fallen condition of man—and applies it to theories of natural rights: "These metaphysic rights entering into common life, like rays of light which pierce into a dense medium, are, by the laws of Nature, refracted from their straight line. Indeed, in the gross and complicated mass of human passions and concerns, the primitive rights of men undergo such a variety of refractions and reflections that it becomes absurd to talk of them as if they continued in the simplicity of their original direction."

These pretended rights, then, share several characteristics. They are abstract, rooted in theories that are easily undone and that invite—perhaps require—abuse if they are to be maintained because they are hostile to human nature. They elevate reason at the expense of feeling, as Burke noted in the *Reflections*: "This sort of people are so taken up with their theories of the rights of man, that they have totally forgot his nature.

Without opening one new avenue to the understanding, they have succeeded in stopping up those that lead to the heart." Because these rights of man are vast and abstract, they make radical claims of transcendence that obviate national borders and local customs. They are hostile to obligation and destructive in character. In the reverse of these qualities, we shall discover what Burke called the "real" or "essential" rights of men.

'The Real Rights of Men"

In his address on conciliation with the colonies, Burke noted that the people of America were not only descendants of Englishmen but also emigrated at a time when the spirit of liberty in the mother country was especially fierce. "They are therefore not only devoted to liberty, but to liberty according to English ideas and on English principles. Abstract liberty, like other mere abstractions, is not to be found. Liberty inheres in some sensible object...." This concreteness anchors rights in a particular political tradition—in the English case, in one in which Burke noted that the "great contests for freedom" had always pertained to taxation. Burke was not willing to resolve the question of American taxation on the grounds of rights. "I am not here going into the distinctions of rights, nor attempting to mark their boundaries," he had said in his Speech on American Taxation. "I do not enter into these metaphysical distinctions; I hate the very sound of them." Instead, Burke counseled Parliament to "revert to your old principles," which were to allow the colonists to tax themselves. Taxation, the root of so many British disputes, was not an issue of rights because it was a matter of positive political arrangements and therefore resided in the realm of prudence. Prudence was exactly the ground on which Burke made his case for conciliation. He would later write to his friend Charles O'Hara about the Speech on Conciliation: "I never ask what Government may do in *Theory*, except *Theory* be the *Object*; When one talks of *Practice* they must act according to circumstances. If you think it worth your while to read that Speech over again you will find that principle to be the Key of it."

As a matter of prudence itself, Burke seemed uncomfortable with the rhetoric of rights growing out of the American rebellion, which he attributed to the widespread study of law in the colonies. (Burke would later write in the *Reflections* that the moment he saw the number of lawyers in the French National Assembly, he foresaw all the violence that was to follow.) He implied in his speech on conciliation with the colonies that the people of America were "mercurial": rather than "judg[ing] of an ill principle in government only by an actual grievance; here they anticipate the evil, and judge of the pressure of the grievance by the badness of the principle. They augur misgovernment at a distance, and snuff the approach of tyranny in every tainted breeze." Importantly, though, Burke felt that these "metaphysical distinctions" were the result, not the cause, of the American dispute. If the British removed the offenses, the claims of rights would recede as well. The case for conciliation with the colonies was, as we have seen, that it was in the public interest of Britain to make the Americans happy. It would be unnatural, he explained, to compel obedience to a throne and Parliament thousands of miles distant over the bitter opposition of disgruntled subjects.

This was neither more nor less than the argument he would later make—and which we have already encountered—with respect to France: that rights, whether of the subject or of the crown, are concrete things to be adjusted prudentially according to circumstances rather than by universal abstractions. He had told the sheriffs of Bristol:

> Civil freedom, Gentlemen, is not, as many have endeavored to persuade you, a thing that lies hid in the depth of abstruse science. It is a blessing and a benefit, not an abstract speculation; and all the just reasoning that can be upon it is of so coarse a texture as perfectly to suit the ordinary capacities of those who are to enjoy, and of those who are to defend it. Far from any resemblance to those propositions in geometry and metaphysics which admit no medium, but must be true or false in all their latitude, social and civil freedom, like all other things in common life, are variously mixed and modified, enjoyed in very different degrees, and shaped into an infinite diversity of forms, according to the temper and circumstances of every community.

Again we see Burke referring rights to the particular disposition of a political community and not to abstract theory. But he also called freedom a "blessing and a benefit," and he was not grudging in allowing for it. It had to be allowed, however, in a social context, which inherently entailed restraint lest it devolve into a war of all against all in which every person's freedom intruded on every other's. He had explained in the 1782 debate on parliamentary reform that "[y]ou admit that there is an extreme in liberty, which may be infinitely noxious to those who are to receive it, and which in the end will leave them no liberty at all. I think so, too." The standard of moderate freedom was to be found in the British constitution because it actually existed and actually protected life, liberty, and property. Under it, "I have that inward and dignified consciousness of my own security and independence, which constitutes, and is the only thing which does constitute, the proud and comfortable sentiment of freedom in the human breast." This "dignified consciousness" of both security and liberty was the result of moderating and limiting them.

The phrase "social freedom," seen in the passage from the letter to the sheriffs of Bristol above, is one Burke defined on another occasion, in the letter to Depont: "[O]f all the loose terms in the world, liberty is the most indefinite. It is not solitary, unconnected, individual, selfish liberty, as if every man was to regulate the whole of his conduct by his own will. The liberty I mean is social freedom. It is that state of things in which liberty is secured by the equality of restraint." The genuine rights of men—Burke was almost always scrupulous to refer to the rights of "men" when he meant to defend them rather than to the French rights of "Man"—inherently entailed restraint. He thus proceeded to tell the sheriffs that "[t]he *extreme* of liberty (which is its abstract perfection, but its real fault) obtains nowhere, nor ought to obtain anywhere.... Liberty, too, must be limited in order to be possessed. The degree of restraint it is impossible in any case to settle precisely." This, again, was a counsel of caution but not of illiberalism. "[I]t ought to be the constant aim of every wise public counsel to find out by cautious experiments, and rational, cool endeavors, with how little, not how much, of this restraint the community can subsist: for liberty is a good to be improved, and not an evil to be lessened." In this context, the end is liberty, while prudence directs limitation and balancing in that direction with a view toward maximizing it.

Limitation and liberty were inescapable companions, so much so that the *Reflections* suggested that boundless liberty was unworthy of the name. Before sacrificing France's material prosperity in pursuit of the Rights of Man, "one ought to be pretty sure it is real liberty which is purchased, and that she is to be purchased at no other price. I shall always, however, consider that liberty as very equivocal in her appearance, which has not wisdom and justice for her companions, and does not lead prosperity and plenty in her train." He explained in his "Letter to a Member of the National Assembly" that "[m]en are qualified for civil liberty in exact proportion to their disposition to put moral chains upon their own appetites...." The liberty of citizens, in other words, entails limits that are self-imposed. The only alternative, the opposite of civil liberty, was for the chains to be imposed by others.

Duties operated alongside limits to impart meaning to liberty. The *Appeal* noted that "men love to hear of their power, but have an extreme disrelish to be told of their duty. This is of course; because every duty is a limitation of some power." In one of the most beautiful and evocative passages in the Burkean corpus, the *Appeal* notes that social, indeed human, life entails the acquisition of duties regardless of whether we contractually choose them: "Dark and inscrutable are the ways by which we come into the world. The instincts which give rise to this mysterious process of Nature are not of our making. But out of physical causes, unknown to us, perhaps unknowable, arise moral duties, which, as we are able perfectly to comprehend, we are bound indispensably to perform." The "Letter to a Member of the National Assembly" therefore said that France's "practical philosophers, systematic in everything, have wisely began at the source"—a formulation dripping in irony and referring to the liberalization of family laws that dissolved ties of obligation. The French ideal of a father, an apparent reference to the substitution of the revolutionary state for the role of parent, was "wild, ferocious, low-minded, hard-hearted...of fine-general feelings,—a lover of his kind, but a hater of his kindred. Your masters reject the duties of this vulgar relation, as contrary to liberty, as not founded in the social compact, and not binding according to the rights of men; because the relation is not, of course, the result of *free election*,—never so on the side of the children, not always on the part of the parents." This emphasis on unchosen but no less sacred duties is also a rejection of social contract theorizing, according to which the isolated individual incurs obligations only by personal choice.

The *Reflections*, which contains Burke's most thoughtful critiques of abstract theories of rights, also supplies some of his most powerful endorsements of liberty well understood. The book, he later wrote to his parliamentary colleague William Weddell, sought to reclaim "a rational and sober Liberty upon the plan of our existing constitution, from those, who think they have no Liberty, if it does not comprehend a right in them of making to themselves new constitutions at their pleasure." The *Reflections* argued that more freedom was better than less, but for the purpose of virtue, not hedonism: "It is better to cherish virtue and humanity, by leaving much to free will, even with some loss to the object, than to attempt to make men mere machines and instruments of a political benevolence. The world on the whole will gain by a liberty without which virtue cannot exist." In the following passage, the *Reflections'* most direct endorsement of civil liberty, rights were adjusted according to the purposes of political society:

> Far am I from denying in theory, full as far is my heart from withholding in practice…the *real* rights of men. In denying their false claims of right, I do not mean to injure those which are real, and are such as their pretended rights would totally destroy. If civil society be made for the advantage of man, all the advantages for which it is made become his right. It is an institution of beneficence; and law itself is only beneficence acting by a rule. Men have a right to live by that rule; they have a right to justice, as between their fellows, whether their fellows are in politic function or in ordinary occupation. They have a right to the fruits of their industry, and to the means of making their industry fruitful. They have a right to the acquisitions of their parents, to the nourishment and improvement of their offspring, to instruction in life and to consolation in death. Whatever each man can separately do, without trespassing upon others, he has a right to do for himself.…

The passage requires careful attention, for it could easily be misread as an endorsement of either utilitarianism ("an institution of beneficence") or libertarianism ("whatever each man can separately do…") if those passages are excerpted from their context. Neither of those labels remotely describes Burke. We have already seen that the "advantages" for which civil society exists are comprehensive: In the famed passage about the generational social compact, it is "a partnership in all science, a partnership in all art, a partnership in every virtue and in all perfection." These advantages did not create positive entitlements but rather, as the liberty to exercise virtue that we have already encountered just above suggests, opportunities. Indeed, what beneficence conferred was a "right" to live according to rules. The *Reflections* elsewhere said that the "advantages" to which men had a right in government "are often in balances between differences of good,—in compromises sometimes between good and evil, and sometimes between evil and evil." Moreover, it is significant that the rights to property, which we shall see were central to Burke's understanding of natural justice, were transgenerational: One had the right to what was left by one's parents, to what one earned oneself, and to leave the fruits of one's labor to one's children. A transgenerational metaphor for the regime operated here as well. As to the superficially libertarian right to do for oneself what does not trespass on others, we have already seen that the realm of purely self-regarding actions was, for Burke, vanishingly small.

Natural Rights

Burke came close in the *Reflections* to suggesting pre-political rights. "[I]t is to the property of the citizen, and not to the demands of the creditor of the state, that the first and original faith of civil society is pledged. The claim of the citizen is prior in time, paramount in title, superior in equity. The fortunes of individuals, whether possessed by acquisition, or by descent, or in virtue of a participation in the goods of some community, were no part of the creditor's security, expressed or implied." He had made a similar argument as early as 1772, when he argued in Parliament that the British government possessed the right to require subscription to the Thirty-Nine Articles of the Church of England for admission to the clergy, from which dissenting ministers had requested an exemption. The distinction he drew was comparable to the one between judicial and prudential matters. Complaints about the subscription resulted from confusing "private judgment, whose rights are anterior to law, and the qualifications which the law creates for its own magistracies, whether civil or religious." It was "tyranny" to take away men's lives, liberty, or property because they were "things for the protection of which society was introduced...." However, "to annex any condition you please to benefits artificially created is the most just, natural, and proper thing in the world."

    It is important not to make too much, or too much of a literal cast, of this rhetoric of a pre-political state, which Burke lampooned in 1756's *A Vindication of Natural Society*. But it is clear he regarded some rights as at least philosophically prior to political society and as natural and universal in character. In the 1782 debate on Fox's East India Bill, Burke denied that reforming the East India Company violated any of the corporation's rights. But in the course of making that argument, he specified: "The rights of *men*—that is to say, the natural rights of mankind—are indeed sacred things; and if any public measure is proved mischievously to affect them, the objection ought to be fatal to that measure, even if no charter at all could be set up against it." The "chartered rights" of specific polities, which the East India Company fallaciously invoked, were liable to violate "the natural rights of mankind at large."

At a minimum, he explained, the exercise of political power, being "a derogation from the natural equality of mankind at large, ought to be some way or other exercised ultimately for their benefit." If he kept a false faith with the East India Company, he would "break the faith, the covenant, the solemn, original, indispensable oath, in which I am bound, by the eternal frame and constitution of things, to the whole human race." This "eternal frame and constitution of things" is very much a transcendent standard of the good, much like the concept of Nature that later commentators like Leo Strauss would accuse Burke of rejecting.

Yet these natural rights were moral rights that all just political institutions were compelled to protect. Again, they were only the most basic, elemental rights and did not touch specific political arrangements except insofar as they were expected to provide, according to local custom, protection for them. Political rights—that is, the rights to specific political arrangements, such as voting or constitutional structures—were the products of inheritance and prescription, and they were regulable for the public good. Even the early English barons did not claim "perfectly free" liberty, Burke wrote in his fragmentary British history, "and they did not claim to possess their privileges upon any natural principle or independent bottom, but just as they held their lands from the king. This is worthy of observation."

Yet having held these lands, they acquired natural status. As Chapter 7 will explain, it was prescription, the law of long usage, that created a natural title to property. The *Reflections* accused the "professors of the rights of men" of being ignorant of the basic fact that "[t]he claim of the citizen [to his property] is prior in time, paramount in title, superior in equity" to the claims of the state. It is significant that this most prominent of rights arose from prescription, which in turn imitated natural processes of long and slow evolution. The *Reflections* explicitly rejected the Lockean idea that "the occupant and subduer of the soil is the true proprietor," a modern claim he located in "the citadel of the rights of men" as opposed to prescription. Prescription, of course, was also rooted in occupation of the soil, but it was seasoned by time, whereas the Rights of Man vacated these titles and invited contemporary men to occupy and subdue anew. The advantage of prescription for property was the same as Chapter 7 will show it was for politics: It imparted stability and justice to an institution that would otherwise be a matter of permanent dispute. Burke defended prescription in a February 1790 letter to his friend Thomas Mercer:

> But these are donations made in "ages of ignorance and superstition." Be it so. It proves that these donations were made long ago; and this is *prescription*; and this gives right and title. It is possible that many estates about you were originally obtained by arms, that is, by violence, a thing almost as bad as superstition, and not much short of ignorance: but it is *old violence*; and that which might be wrong in the beginning, is consecrated by time, and becomes lawful. This may be superstition in me, and ignorance; but I had rather remain in ignorance and superstition than be enlightened and purified out of the first principles of law and natural justice.

These natural rights, then, are the simplest, most basic guarantees, grounded in processes of nature itself. They partake of a moral character, and an infinite variety of political arrangements are capable of protecting them. But the protections remain. This is most evident in what Burke, in a 1796 letter to his friend French Laurence, called his "monument": his long campaign for the rights of the people of India, culminating in his years-long impeachment of Warren Hastings, the former governor-general of India.

"The Essential Principles of Natural Justice": The Hastings Impeachment

Hastings was accused of profuse corruption but also of far worse. The articles of impeachment charged him with operating a scheme of arbitrary government that employed murder, torture, and plunder to extract wealth from the royalty and peasantry of India. Hastings had laid waste to the country, degraded its noblemen, and disgraced its noblewomen, and done so while claiming the people of India had no rights. "I mean to prove the direct contrary of everything that has been said on this subject by the prisoner's counsel, or by himself," Burke said later in the trial. "I mean to prove that the people of India have laws, rights, and immunities; that they have property, movable and immovable, descendible as well as occasional; that they have property held for life, and that they have it as well secured to them by the laws of their country as any property is secured in this country...." In his affecting peroration opening the Hastings impeachment, Burke declared clearly that he was not confining himself merely to the canons of positive law. He was starting there, but would proceed to the fundamentals of justice itself:

> I impeach him in the name of all the Commons of Great Britain, whose national character he has dishonored. I impeach him in the name of the people of India, whose laws, rights, and liberties he has subverted, whose properties he has destroyed, whose country he has laid waste and desolate. I impeach him in the name and by virtue of those eternal laws of justice which he has violated. I impeach him in the name of human nature itself, which he has cruelly outraged, injured, and oppressed, in both sexes, in every age, rank, situation, and condition of life.

The impeachment managers, he explained, would almost always meet the standard of evidence necessary for a conviction at criminal trial, but that was not the standard of impeachment, in which statesmen judged the actions of statesmen. Thus, "you are not bound by any rules of evidence, or any other rules whatever, except those of natural, immutable, and substantial justice."

Throughout the impeachment, which lasted years, Burke would return again and again to this rhetoric of transcendent principles of justice. Hastings's administration "was one whole system of oppression, of robbery of individuals...in order to defeat the ends which all governments ought in common to have in view." Hastings, he remarked separately in the trial, had discretionary power but "was bound to use that power according to the established rules of political morality, humanity, and equity." That rule, he would later suggest, was "that all discretion must be referred to the conservation and benefit of those over whom power is exercised, and therefore must be guided by rules of sound political morality."

What were these "eternal laws of justice," and, more important, how could we distinguish them from the French Rights of Man? We have already seen that the despoiling of property, which formed a substantial part of Burke's prosecution of Hastings, violated a natural process. But he also suggested these offenses presented themselves directly to the faculty of the feelings. "[F]or years [Hastings] lay down in that sty of disgrace, fattening in it, feeding upon that offal of disgrace and excrement, upon everything that could be disgustful to the human mind...." Late in the trial, responding to Hastings' counsel, he told the House of Lords:

> My Lords, if there is a spark of manhood, if there is in your breasts the
> least feeling for our common humanity, and especially for the sufferings
> and distresses of that part of human nature which is made by its peculiar
> constitution more quick and sensible,—if, I say, there is a trace of this
> in your breasts, if you are yet alive to such feelings, it is impossible that
> you should not join with the Commons of Great Britain in feeling the
> utmost degree of indignation against the man who was the guilty cause
> of this accumulated distress.

Burke proceeded to say that justice "defies all mutation" and that God had placed it in every human heart to guide us with respect to ourselves and others. The injustices that present themselves immediately to our hearts include the degradation of the ennobled but also the plunder of an entire people and the arbitrary exercise of power. Burke was shocked that Hastings claimed that the people of India "have no liberty, no laws, no inheritance, no fixed property, no descendable estate, no subordinations in society, no sense of honor or of shame, and that they are affected by punishment so far as punishment is a corporal infliction, being totally insensible of any difference between the punishment of man and beast." We have here a distillation of the power but also the limited scope of Burke's moral conception of natural rights. There are rights to regulable liberty, to the rule of law, to basic dignity, and the like. None of these assert total equality, obliterate old customs—on the contrary, such customs would be affirmed by these rights—or guarantee specific political arrangements. Arbitrary power was incompatible with all this, Burke explained; it was "treason in the law" and "a contradiction in terms." The effects were felt, he explained, not just in India but also when young Englishmen were corrupted by this system and returned to the mother country with ill-gotten wealth and insinuated themselves into the aristocracy and political system of Great Britain. "Good God! My Lords, if you are not appalled with the violent injustice of arbitrary proceedings, you must feel something humiliating at the gross ignorance of men who are in this manner playing with the rights of mankind."

Rights as Prudence: The Liberties of Ireland

The rights Burke asserted in India were basic but universal. His lifelong and deeply personal crusade for the rights of Catholics in his native Ireland showed how liberty could also take on a prudential dimension. Discrimination against Catholics took several forms. Trade with Ireland had been restricted, and Irish Catholics had been placed under severe political and educational restrictions. Burke opposed them all. We have already seen him argue, even as he pushed for the fullest religious toleration, that the British government was within its rights to require subscription to the Thirty-Nine Articles of the Church of England. Yet it was imprudent, he relentlessly argued, to oppress Irish Catholics. He wrote to the Irish Viscount Kenmare in 1782's "Letter to a Peer of Ireland" that the anti-Catholic laws were a foolish attempt "to sacrifice the civil prosperity of the Nation to its religious improvement." This latter goal could hardly be achieved by coercion and penalty.

Far from it: Burke later argued that continued repression would shove Irish Catholics into the arms of Jacobinism, corrupt the oppressing Protestantism, and serve no constructive purpose. Conor Cruise O'Brien has argued that there was a personal element to this crusade: that Burke had secretly converted to the Roman Catholicism practiced by both his mother and his wife. The evidence for this hypothesis is ultimately both inconclusive and unnecessary to explain Burke's views on religious toleration, which he felt served the prudential interests of England and Ireland alike. When an iron firm in his Bristol parliamentary district complained of his support for liberalizing Irish trade, he replied by letter in 1778 that his duty, and their interest, lay in the good of the entire kingdom: "It is *for* you, and *for* your Interest, as a dear, cherished, and respected part of a valuable whole, that I have taken my share in this question."

In a move we have seen is essential to his view of prudence, Burke denied that the measures taken against Catholics at the time of the Glorious Revolution created precedents justifying oppression descending to his day. He wrote Langrishe: "As in most great changes, many things were done from the necessities of the time, well or ill understood, from passion or from vengeance, which were not only not perfectly agreeable to its principles, but in the most direct contradiction to them." The particular cruelty of these measures—which Burke characterized in a speech before the 1780 parliamentary election in Bristol as the early Reformation's initial impulse "to oppose to Popery another Popery" with laws "as bloody as any of those which had been enacted by the Popish princes and states"—was that they "kept men alive only to insult in their persons every one of the rights and feelings of mankind."

He wrote to Langrishe that the purpose of the "Popery Laws" penalizing Catholics was to divide Ireland between possessors and the dispossessed. "Are we to be astonished, when, by the efforts of so much violence in conquest, and so much policy in regulation, continued without intermission for near an hundred years, we had reduced them to a mob that, whenever they came to act, many of them would act exactly like a mob, without temper, measure, or foresight?" Still, he warned, the answer was not a new constitution resulting in a "frantic democracy," but rather prudential balancing:

> Between the extreme of a *total exclusion,* to which your maxim goes, and *an universal unmodified capacity,* to which the fanatics pretend, there are many different degrees and stages, and a great variety of temperaments, upon which prudence may give full scope to its exertions. For you know that the decisions of prudence (contrary to the system of the insane reasoners) differ from those of judicature; and that almost all the former are determined on the more or the less, the earlier or the later, and on a balance of advantage and inconvenience, of good and evil.

Religious toleration was as important to the state as uprooting atheism, for it was part of the maintenance of religion itself. Burke cast this in prudential terms. "At the same time that I would cut up the very root of atheism, I would respect all conscience,—all conscience that is really such, and which perhaps its very tenderness proves to be sincere," he told Parliament in 1773. That suggests room for prudential judgment in assessing the sincerity of religious belief, which Burke did in rejecting the petition of the Unitarian Society as a thin veneer placed over the political creed of Jacobinism. One measure of sincerity was prescription. He thus wrote to William Burgh, then a member of the Irish Parliament, in 1775, that he would extend "a full civil protection" to Jews, Muslims, "and even Pagans; especially if they are already possessed of any of those advantages by long and prescriptive usage; which is as sacred in this exercise of Rights, as in any other." Religious toleration was a part of religion itself, he said in the 1773 address. "I do not know which I would sacrifice: I would keep them both: it is not necessary I should sacrifice either."

Burke decried Irish Protestant assertions of a right to suppress the religious practices of Irish Catholics as "not freedom but dominion" that would corrupt those who exercised it. The bitter thread of consistency through British politics, he wrote to the Rev. Thomas Hussey in Ireland in 1796, was that Catholics were being oppressed as Britain made peace with the Revolutionary French: "Defeat and dishonor abroad; Oppression at Home—We sneak to the Regicides, but we boldly trample upon our fellow Citizens. But all is for the Protestant Cause." Those who oppressed the Irish did so selfishly, not for the souls of the oppressed but because they relished oppressing them: "I am sure I have known those who have oppressed Papists in their civil rights exceedingly indulgent to them in their religious ceremonies, and who really wished them to continue Catholics, in order to furnish pretences for oppression," he wrote in his 1782 "Letter to a Peer of Ireland" on the Catholic penal laws. "These persons never saw a man (by converting) escape out of their power, but with grudging and regret."

Some Protestants excavated the supposed ancient sins of Catholics who had participated in a 1641 rebellion to justify continued repressive measures. Burke, writing to his son in 1793, replied prudentially:

What lesson does the iniquity of prevalent factions read to us? It ought to lesson us into an abhorrence of the abuse of our own power in our own day, when we hate its excesses so much in other persons and in other times. To that school true statesmen ought to be satisfied to leave mankind. They ought not to call from the dead all the discussions and litigations which formerly inflamed the furious factions which had torn their country to pieces; they ought not to rake into the hideous and abominable things which were done in the turbulent fury of an injured, robbed, and persecuted people, and which were afterwards cruelly revenged in the execution, and as outrageously and shamefully exaggerated in the representation, in order, an hundred and fifty years after, to find some color for justifying them in the eternal proscription and civil excommunication of a whole people.

This "moral imagination"—the ability to project ourselves into the situation of others—was a technique Lincoln often employed to challenge the institution of slavery.

CHAPTER SIX

☙ ❧

As I Would Not Be a Slave, So I Would Not Be a Master

Lincoln on Liberty

When Lincoln called Congress into special session at the onset of the Civil War, he sought immediately to define the conflict. His message to legislators explained: "This is essentially a People's contest. On the side of the Union, it is a struggle for maintaining in the world, that form, and substance of government, whose leading object is, to elevate the condition of men—to lift artificial weights from all shoulders—to clear the paths of laudable pursuit for all—to afford all, an unfettered start, and a fair chance, in the race of life." A great deal is latent in this passage. In perhaps the clearest divergence between Burke and Lincoln, it cast the war in universalist terms: It was about maintaining principles not just at home but also "in the world." The idea of elevation—of lifting people up—was closely related to the connection Lincoln drew between rights and progress, evident here in "the paths of laudable pursuit." Yet this defense of honest labor was sober and decidedly non-utopian.

Most significant, even this early in the war, when Lincoln's understanding of the conflict pertained to the maintenance of constitutional union and when he did not yet contemplate abolishing slavery where it existed—an outcome the Second Inaugural would later call "astounding"—he understood a "People's" war in terms of lifting burdens from individuals' shoulders. Slavery was such a burden, not just to enslaved people but to all, especially the free laboring classes. Finally, it bears emphasis that Lincoln promised no more than "an unfettered start, and a fair chance" in life. His view of liberty could be so universal in reach because it was so fundamental in scope. In this sense, what Lincoln sometimes called "natural rights" resemble Burke's nature as well.

All this added up to a "People's" war—not one of individual rights sequestered from the public square or of popular rights uncontrolled by personal liberty. To see why, we must confront, as this chapter will, Lincoln's complex understanding of democracy as encompassing both. "As I would not be a slave, so I would not be a master," Lincoln wrote around 1858 in a note on slavery and democracy. "This expresses my idea of democracy. Whatever differs from this, to the extent of the difference, is no democracy." This is an intuitively appealing idea of democracy, but it requires closer inspection. Typically democracy is a principle of decision: rule by the many. Lincoln, operating on what Weaver calls the "argument from definition," transformed it into a normative standard into which a great deal—political equality and self-rule, among other values—is compressed. He had done so in other contexts as well, such as the 1839 speech on the Sub-Treasury Plan, which he said "benefit[ted] the few at the expense of the many.... And was the sacred name of Democracy, ever before made to endorse such an enormity against the rights of the people?" Lincolnian democracy, as we shall see, was a universal value, but was limited in its claims. It was an agent, but did not make an idol, of progress. It reconciled the values of popular rule and personal rights.

In his special message to Congress on July 4, 1861, Lincoln noted that the Confederate constitution spoke in the idiom of "We, the deputies of the sovereign and independent States" rather than "We, the people." He wondered: "Why? Why this deliberate pressing out of view, the rights of men and the authority of the people?" In contemporary terms, we are accustomed to place these two values—the rights of individuals and the authority of the community—at loggerheads. Lincoln's denunciation of Douglas's doctrine of "popular sovereignty," which would have allowed each new state to decide for itself whether to accept or reject slavery, invites us in many ways to do so. But for Lincoln, there was no such conflict, which was why he opened the Gettysburg Address with the promise of "liberty" and ended it with a devotion to "government of the people, by the people, for the people." His "idea of democracy" was that individuals and communities could simultaneously rule themselves.

Lincoln's understanding of liberty was unquestionably more capacious than Burke's. We should expect the conceptions of each to be shaped by the constitutional traditions they inherited. Lincoln's Constitution was both written and at least more specific as to rights, while Burke's was traditional and unwritten. While both thinkers found slavery repulsive, Burke rejected a wide-ranging conception of equality as an operating principle of politics. Lincoln was likelier to speak in axioms and universals than in terms of inheritances and customs. Yet there are also linkages, most especially in those areas that connect liberty with the anchoring principle of prudence. Both located their ideas of liberty not just in reason, but in sentiment. Lincoln, as we shall see, confined his use of moral abstraction to the political situation in which it was appropriate and, indeed, unavoidable: the organization of new governments in the territories. Each saw liberty as an agent of improvement. Most important, in the French Revolution and Civil War respectively, Burke and Lincoln recognized dangers to liberty in their times as ultimate issues demanding ultimate responses—a calibration of action to circumstance that is the essence of prudence.

"A Moral, Social and Political Evil"

It was particularly vexing to Lincoln when apologists for slavery professed indifference to the institution. "This *declared* indifference" was actually "covert *real* zeal for the spread of slavery," which Lincoln "hate[d]," he said at Peoria, because it replaced the truths of the Declaration with the claim that "there is no right principle of action but *self-interest.*" The Democratic Party had attempted to maintain this neutrality until the *Dred Scott* decision, whereupon, Lincoln said in Edwardsville, Illinois, in September 1858, it had endorsed the perverse notion "that slavery is *better* than freedom."

Importantly, the wrongness of slavery presented itself not just to the understanding but also to human sympathy. As we have seen, hundreds of thousands of free African Americans in the country were descendants of freed slaves, not property. Why were they freed, he asked at Peoria? "In all these cases it is your sense of justice, and human sympathy, continually telling you, that the poor negro has some natural right to himself...." Lincoln accused Douglas of lacking that sympathy, remarking in Columbus, Ohio, in September 1859 that his adversary was "so put up by nature that a lash upon his back would hurt him, but a lash upon anybody else's back does not hurt him. That is the build of the man, and consequently he looks upon the matter of slavery in this unimportant light." That was not Lincoln's build. He felt the injustice of slavery with genuine anguish. He told the 140th Indiana Regiment in March 1865 that everyone should be free, "but if any should be slaves it should be first those who desire it for *themselves*, and secondly those who *desire* it for *others*. Whenever [I] hear any one, arguing for slavery I feel a strong impulse to see it tried on him personally."

This sympathy was one important reason that there was no gainsaying slavery: One had to declare on it, a responsibility Douglas had somehow escaped. "There is not a public man in the United States, I believe, with the exception of Senator Douglas, who has not, at some time in his life, declared his opinion whether the thing is right or wrong," Lincoln said in Cincinnati in 1859, "but, Senator Douglas never declares it is wrong." Lincoln did. He characterized the Republican position as the belief that slavery was "a moral, social and political wrong" that had to be confronted in all these respects. "I suggest," he said in the Lincoln-Douglas debate at Quincy, "that the difference of opinion, reduced to its lowest terms, is no other than the difference between the men who think slavery a wrong and those who do not think it wrong." At the next debate, in Quincy, he expanded on the theme. "It is the eternal struggle between these two principles—right and wrong—throughout the world. They are the two principles that have stood face to face from the beginning of time; and will ever continue to struggle." Like Burke, Lincoln was not eager to declare all issues to be ultimate, but he knew an ultimate issue when he saw one. At New Haven in 1860, he recognized that pro-slavery forces would broach no compromise. Nothing would convince them but to "cease to call slavery *wrong*, and [to] join them in calling it *right*." Unless Republicans were willing to say the opposite—to call slavery wrong and to do so unapologetically, he explained at Cooper Union—they had no grounds for refusing to recognize the institution nationally: "Nor can we justifiably withhold [our approval], on any ground save our conviction that slavery is wrong."

For Lincoln, opposition to slavery arose not simply from his sympathy for enslaved people but also from his concern about its corrosive effects on everyone it touched. He said at Edwardsville that slavery was "an unqualified evil to the negro, to the white man, to the soil, and to the State." This was true in several respects. One, he continued at Edwardsville, was that there was no guarantee that the grim logic of dehumanization and suppression would not be turned on whites next if the principles of liberty were undermined. "This is a world of compensations," he wrote to Henry L. Pierce in 1859 in the language of prudence, "and he who would *be* no slave, must consent to *have* no slave." This simple ethic of natural justice was the same one that had impelled him to define democracy as the belief that he could not be a master because he would not be a slave. Lincoln said in New Haven that the same arguments used to defend slavery eroded the foundations of free government for everyone. Moreover, enslaved labor competed unfairly with free labor, such that, he said at Cincinnati in 1859, "the mass of white men are really injured by the effect of slave labor in the vicinity of the fields of their own labor." Laboring whites had as much claim to the new territories as anyone, he said in Dayton, Ohio, in September 1859, and they "should not be placed in a position where, by the introduction of slavery into the territories, [they] would be compelled to toil by the side of a slave." Democracy and slavery could not coexist, especially on Lincoln's broad understanding of what democracy entailed.

To somehow fuse slavery and democracy, it was necessary for slavery's defenders to deprive African Americans of their humanity. Lincoln explained in New Haven that this dehumanization appeared suddenly, of necessity, with the Kansas-Nebraska Act: "Four or five years ago we all thought negroes were men, and that when '*all men*' were named [in the Declaration], negroes were included. But *the whole Democratic party has deliberately taken negroes from the class of men and put them in the class of brutes.*" In Janesville, Wisconsin, in October 1859, he systematically dismantled Douglas's claim that he would choose the white man over the African American but the African American over a crocodile: "Or the matter might be put in this shape: As the white man is to the negro, so is the negro to the crocodile!" The particular tragedy of this position was its assumption of racial conflict, "or that the freedom of the white man

was insecure unless the negro was reduced to a state of abject slavery....
[A]s long as his tongue could utter a word [Lincoln said] he would com-
bat that infamous idea. There was room for all races and as there was no
conflict so there was no necessity of getting up an excitement in relation
to it." It bears emphasis that Lincoln, again acting prudentially, attempted
to defuse conflict before the issue reached an ultimate point from which
there was no turning back.

"The Rights of Human Nature"

Universalism appeared in Lincoln's rhetoric on liberty almost from the
beginning. It was not messianic, but neither did Lincoln limit liberty
to Burke's "entailed inheritance" specific to each community. This was
evident as early as the Temperance Address of 1842. In the American
Revolution, he said, "the world has found a solution of that long mooted
problem, as to the capability of man to govern himself. In it was the germ
which has vegetated, and still is to grow and expand into the universal
liberty of mankind." In the Peoria Address, one reason he deplored moral
indifference to slavery was that it "deprives our republican example of its
just influence in the world...."

In response to a supportive message from the workingmen of London,
Lincoln wrote in 1863 that the Civil War had put the very viability of
these ideas to the test. "It seems to have devolved upon [Americans] to
test whether a government, established on the principles of human freedom, can be maintained against an effort to build one upon the exclusive
foundation of human bondage." That November, he repeated the idea at
Gettysburg: "Now we are engaged in a great civil war, testing whether that
nation, or any nation so conceived and so dedicated, can long endure." It
is worth asking why "any" government built on the ideals of equality and
consent would face a particular challenge to its viability. On Lincoln's
understanding, until the American experiment, governments had generally been based on fear. As he had recognized in the Lyceum Address's
call for reverence for the laws to be made into a "political religion," the
unique challenge of a republic was that it was knit together by ideals
rather than force.

These ideals, in contrast to Burke, were less inheritable than proposi-
tional; better put, anyone who subscribed to them could become an heir

to them. For this reason, the Declaration of Independence guaranteed rights to immigrants as much as to direct descendants of the American Revolution. The Declaration was, he told a Chicago audience in July 1858, "the electric cord…that links the hearts of patriotic and liberty-loving men together, that will link those patriotic hearts as long as the love of freedom exists in the minds of men throughout the world." This is something of a curious conjunction: "Patriotism" suggests belonging to a particular political community, as do Lincoln's frequent references to "civil" liberty, that is, the liberty of citizens, yet the passage ends with a reference to "men throughout the world." The prudential bridge between them is that Lincoln limited his universalism to the power of American example. A patriotic defense of American liberty could guide other liberty-loving people around the world.

These propositions were "abstract"; they were, he would write to the Swedish minister Edward Count Piper in November 1861, "the rights of human nature and the capacity of man for self-government," just as he replied to an address from the laborers of Manchester, England, in 1863 that the American government "was built upon the foundation of human rights" as opposed to human slavery. The axioms of the Declaration, he wrote to Pierce, represented "an abstract truth, applicable to all men and all times…." The Declaration gave liberty "not alone to the people of this country," he said at Independence Hall en route to his inauguration, "but hope to the world for all future time. It was that which gave promise that in due time the weights should be lifted from the shoulders of all men, and that *all* should have an equal chance." Again, the Declaration gave the precise contours of liberty to this political community and the *hope* for liberty to the world, all of whose people would be liberated, but only "in due time."

Liberated from what? The answer was from chains of despotism that inhibited self-government—no less, but also no more. Lincoln's idea of natural right, like Burke's, had immovable but limited, and thus prudential, content. To say it was limited is not to deny its vitality; it was, after all, as vital as the difference between freedom and slavery, whether those terms were understood politically or personally. Lincoln's idea of equal rights was not equality in all things. Even as he sought to elevate public attitudes toward African Americans, as we have seen Diana Schaub demonstrate, it was politically necessary for Lincoln to deny that he believed in full social equality—necessary in the sense that he could have moved no further toward the attainment of more fundamental rights had he reached too high, too quickly, for total rights. Even so, at Chicago in 1858, Lincoln stopped short of repudiating equality, instead qualifying his remark with "perhaps": "Certainly the negro is not our equal in color—perhaps not in many other respects; still, in the right to put into his mouth the bread that his own hands have earned, he is the equal of every other man, white or black." This characterization—denying equality in color but avoiding a definitive disparagement of its more specific dimensions—was Lincoln's consistent practice, as in the first Lincoln-Douglas debate. "Judge Douglas, [the African American] is not my equal in many respects—certainly not in color, perhaps not in moral or intellectual endowment. But in the right to eat the bread, without leave of anybody else, which his own hand earns, *he is my equal and the equal of Judge Douglas, and the equal of every living man.*" This single word—"perhaps"—contains an immense statement on Lincoln's statesmanship and character. He could not have gone further. Going as far as to qualify the statement in that crucial respect required immense courage.

Those who did fully repudiate racial equality were under a special obligation to African Americans, Lincoln argued. To say they should be treated harshly on grounds of inferiority was to reverse Christian charity. In a note on "Pro-slavery Theology" around 1858, Lincoln wrote: "Suppose it is true, that the negro is inferior to the white, in the gifts of nature; is it not the exact reverse [of] justice that the white should, for that reason, take from the negro, any part of the little which has been given him? '*Give to him that is needy*' is the Christian rule of charity; but 'Take from him that is needy' is the rule of slavery." The same year, he told an audience in Springfield, "All I ask for the negro is that if you do not like him, let him alone. If God gave him but little, that little let him enjoy."

Lincoln could play this equality card cleverly. While he disclaimed a belief in full racial equality, he also turned the tables on the free majority by saying he allowed that the people of Nebraska, whose "right" to choose slavery Douglas defended, were "as good as the average of people elsewhere." Lincoln explained at Peoria that he had never denied Nebraskans' full moral equality. "What I do say is, that no man is good enough to govern another man, *without that other's consent*. I say this is the leading principle—the sheet anchor of American republicanism."

Notice the reversal. While positive defenders of slavery had retreated to the argument that it was justified by African American inferiority, Lincoln demanded that the slaveholder demonstrate his superiority to a degree that would justify ruling over another. Further, the only fundamental right Lincoln had claimed was consent, which operated both politically—through majority rule constitutionally expressed—and personally, through his refusal to acknowledge the right of property in people. The convergence of these dimensions of consent constitutes a grounding and prudential standard of "republicanism."

In an 1857 draft speech, Lincoln expanded this personal right to self-government, rejecting once more the idea that it included "the privilege one man takes of making a slave of another...."What it meant to Lincoln, instead, was this: "I am for the people of the whole nation doing just as they please in all matters which concern the whole nation; for those of each part doing just as they choose in all matters which concern no other part; and for each individual doing just as he chooses in all matters which concern nobody else." At his 1864 remarks at a Sanitary Fair in Baltimore, Lincoln noted that "[t]he world has never had a good definition of the word liberty, and the American people, just now, are much in want of one....With some the word liberty may mean for each man to do as he pleases with himself, and the product of his labor; while with others the same word may mean for some men to do as they please with other men, and the product of other men's labor."

This authority of national majorities to decide national issues was why, consistent with his theory of minority rights, Lincoln could demolish Douglas's doctrine of popular sovereignty. The naturally expansionist character of slavery made it a national issue, not a local one.

Personal Rights and Popular Sovereignty

Lincoln's critique of popular sovereignty has led to misunderstandings of him as a natural-rights critic of majority rule. In fact, Lincoln was a majoritarian for whom the crucial question was at what level of government majorities should decide. In 1848, addressing the House of Representatives on the Mexican War, Lincoln proclaimed a right of any people to rebel and, in fact, of a majority of such a people to compel a minority among them to go along. "Such minority, was precisely the case, of the tories of our own revolution." In the First Inaugural, he decried secession as a repudiation of majority rule. "A majority, held in restraint by constitutional checks, and limitations, and always changing easily, with deliberate changes of popular opinions and sentiments, is the only true sovereign of a free people." Communities divided into majorities and minorities on all questions within the scope of the Constitution, he explained. "If the minority will not acquiesce, the majority must, or the government must cease. There is no other alternative; for continuing the government, is acquiescence on one side or the other." Just before the 1864 presidential election, Lincoln told a serenading crowd in Washington that the people had the right to give up the war if they deliberately chose to do so. "[I] know not the power or the right to resist them," he said. "It is their own business, and they must do as they please with their own." Lincoln's belief in democracy as a system rooted in constitutional majority rule blended with personal freedom contrasts substantially with Burke's endorsement of a mixed regime. Burke, too, believed in a popular element in government, but only an element. As Bourke has observed, what mattered to him was "an equality of liberty under government" rather than "the equal exercise of the levers of government." In a sense, Burke straddled a moment in history spanning the old aristocratic regimes of Europe and the emerging democratic ethos of Lincoln's world. Burke clung to the former; Lincoln knew only the latter.

To see how this belief in popular rule was compatible with Lincoln's critique of popular sovereignty, we must understand why, to Lincoln, slavery in the territories was inherently a matter of national concern, to be submitted to national rather than local majorities. Lincoln saw this immediately upon the passage of the Kansas-Nebraska Act in 1854, and the *Dred Scott* ruling in 1857—which overturned the Missouri Compromise on the grounds that Congress had no authority to restrict slavery in the territories—confirmed it. A Supreme Court that prevented Congress from barring slavery in the territories could just as easily inhibit states from barring it within their own borders. All that was necessary to nationalize slavery, he said at the first Lincoln-Douglas debate, was "the next Dred Scott decision. It is merely for the Supreme Court to decide that no *State* under the Constitution can exclude it, just as they have already decided that under the Constitution neither Congress nor the Territorial Legislature can do it."

For Lincoln, the expansion of slavery into new territories or states was not an appropriate question for local "popular sovereignty" because its implications were inherently national. This was partly because Lincoln felt slavery was a naturally expansionist institution with an insatiable appetite for more territory. At the Lincoln-Douglas debate at Galesburg, as we have seen, he explained that if Douglas's conception of popular sovereignty prevailed, "the next thing will be a grab for the territory of poor Mexico, an invasion of the rich lands of South America, then the adjoining islands will follow, each one of which promises additional slave fields." Slavery was a wrong whose tendency was to "exten[d] itself to the existence of the whole nation," he said at the next debate, in Quincy. Lincoln also noted slavery's propensity to establish itself ineradicably and rend the political fabric of the whole nation. He told a Columbus, Ohio, audience in September 1859 that Douglas's idea of "squatter sovereignty" depended on the idea "that slavery is one of those little, unimportant, trivial matters which are of just about as much consequence" as what a neighboring farmer planted. Douglas held

> that when a new territory is opened for settlement, the first man who goes into it may plant there a thing which, like the Canada thistle, or some other of those pests of the soil, cannot be dug out by the millions of men who will come thereafter; that it is one of those little things that is so trivial in its nature that it has no effect upon anybody save the few men who first plant upon the soil; that it is not a thing which in any way affects the family of communities composing these States, nor any way endangers the general government. Judge Douglas ignores altogether the very well known fact, that we have never had a serious menace to our political existence, except it sprang from this thing which he chooses to regard as only upon a par with onions and potatoes.

More important, in the question of slavery in the territories, Lincoln confronted a situation Burke never did: the formation of governments genuinely from scratch, without prescriptive practices to use as an anchoring guide. As a result, they differed fundamentally from states in which slavery was already long established and difficult to uproot. In those states, Lincoln explained in New Haven, slavery was "tolerable only because, and so far as its actual existence makes it necessary to tolerate it...." This was a prudent concession to circumstance. But in situations in which new governments were being formed and slavery was not yet established, Lincoln held, proceeding on abstract moral reasoning was appropriate. This was an equally prudent recognition that the circumstances on the ground in these territories differed. In Galesburg, he explained that his proclamations on slavery referred

> to the abstract moral question, to contemplate and consider when we are legislating about any new country which is not already cursed with the actual presence of the evil—slavery. I have never manifested any impatience with the necessities that spring from the actual presence of black people amongst us, and the actual existence of slavery amongst us where it does already exist; but I have instead that, in legislating for new countries, where it does not exist, there is no just rule other than that of moral and abstract right!

For this reason, he had argued in Springfield in October 1854, the authors of the Northwest Ordinance of 1787—"the founders of liberty and republicanism on this continent"—had denied the new territories the very popular sovereignty Douglas now sought to claim as a basic right. In Janesville, he said that "the public mind had become debauched by the popular sovereignty dogma of Judge Douglas," a belief that was wholly new until the Kansas-Nebraska Act. He had similarly said in the Peoria Address that the idea of self-government was being perversely invoked: "That *perfect* liberty they sigh for—the liberty of making slaves of other people—Jefferson never thought of; their own father never thought of; they never thought of themselves, a year ago. How fortunate for them, they did not sooner become sensible of their great misery!" This was an implicit appeal to the authority of tradition, which we shall confront more fully in Chapter 7. This "perfect" liberty, which was of course neither perfect nor liberty, found no basis in American history, either remotely or recently. It was a new discovery based on the sudden claim that slavery was a positive good and a personal right.

Genuine popular sovereignty entailed both consent at the appropriate level of government and a personal right of consent that the slaveholder denied the enslaved person. This was where Lincoln's political and personal conceptions of democracy converged. Lincoln self-consciously sought to turn popular sovereignty against itself by showing that allowing some people to make slaves of others was not an exercise but rather a repudiation of popular sovereignty.

"[A]ccording to our ancient faith, the just powers of governments are derived from the consent of the governed," he said in Peoria. "Now the relation of masters and slaves is, PRO TANTO, a total violation of this principle.... Allow ALL the governed an equal voice in the government, and that, and that only is self-government." Genuine popular sovereignty, Lincoln explained in Edwardsville in September 1858, was a timeless truth that preceded even Columbus's landing in the New World. But prudence realizes the abstract through the concrete, as did Lincoln: The Declaration gave this axiom "tangible form" and "applied [it] to the American people" through the idea of consent. "If that is not Popular Sovereignty, then I have no conception of the meaning of words."

Consensus as to these kinds of principles, and not merely formal laws, was necessary to prevent the spread or even nationalization of slavery. Lincoln was always eager, as we have already seen, to establish political practice on the basis of what the Lyceum Address had called "sober reason." The best and, ultimately, only safeguard against the expansion of slavery was an understanding that it was wrong. In notes he wrote for speeches around August 1858, Lincoln observed that if Douglas succeeded in "moulding public sentiment" to his own views—which included silence on the wrong of slavery and a willingness to enslave the weak while believing that doing so was the epitome of liberty—"when, I say, public sentiment shall be brought to all this, in the name of heaven, what barrier will be left against slavery being made lawful every where?"

Rights and Progress

Rights were also, for Lincoln, an agent of progress, understood in the terms in which we have already encountered it in Chapter 4: not as an idol unto itself, one rooted in human perfectibility, but rather one rising from steady improvement and personal activity. This was sober rather than utopian progress. His circa 1854 "Fragments on Government" characterized tyranny as the belief that some men were too ignorant to "share in government" and consequently should be kept that way. By contrast, Americans "proposed to give *all* a chance; and we expected the weak to grow stronger, the ignorant, wiser; and all better, and happier together. We made the experiment; and the fruit is before us. Look at it—think of it. Look at it, in its aggregate grandeur, of extent of country, and numbers of population—of ship, and steamboat, and rail—"

This freedom and progress arose from the principle that "[i]n all that the people can individually do as well for themselves, government ought not to interfere." He returned to this theme in his January 1861 "Fragment on the Constitution and Union," tracing the cause of American prosperity further back from the Constitution and the Union to the principles of the Declaration. "There is something back of these, entwining itself more closely about the human heart. That something, is the principle of 'Liberty to all'—the principle that clears the *path* for all—gives *hope* to all—and, by consequence, *enterprize*, and *industry* to all." Again we see the prudential expression of the abstract in concrete circumstance. Had that principle not been expressed, the American revolutionaries would have had no cause for which to fight, and the subsequent progress could not have been attained. Speaking to the 148th Ohio Regiment in August 1864, Lincoln marveled that "[t]o the humblest and poorest among us are held out the highest privileges and ambitions. The present moment finds me at the White House, yet there is as good a chance for your children as there was for my father's."

This progress was inseparable from the Republican philosophy of "free soil, free labor, free men," which sought to anchor individual initiative in the ability of each person to prosper from the fruits of his or her own toil. Lincoln explained in Kalamazoo, Michigan, in August 1856: "We stand at once the wonder and admiration of the whole world, and we must enquire what it is that has given us so much prosperity, and we shall understand that to give up that one thing, would be to give up all future prosperity. This cause is that every man can make himself. It has been said that such a race of prosperity has been run nowhere else." Apologists for slavery who insisted that enslaved people lived better than free Northerners did not understand the importance to the latter of the possibility of advancement. These apologists "think that men are always to remain laborers here—but there is no such class. The man who labored for another last year, this year labors for himself, and next year he will hire others to labor for him."

Addressing the Wisconsin State Agricultural Society in September 1859, Lincoln explained this "free labor" system, which emphasized thrift and hard work. Under it, "[i]f any continue through life in the condition of the hired laborer, it is not the fault of the system, but because of either a dependent nature which prefers it, or improvidence, folly, or singular misfortune." The free labor system made it necessary for educated people to work and, importantly, thereby made education and labor compatible. By contrast, the "mud-sill" theory of labor, which formed the philosophical basis of slavery, held that the ideal laborer was "a blind horse upon a tread-mill...all the better for being blind, that he could not tread out of place, or kick understandingly. According to that theory, the education of laborers, is not only useless, but pernicious, and dangerous." The laboring classes were especially to be praised, Lincoln told Congress in his December 1861 Annual Message: "No men living are more worthy to be trusted than those who toil up from poverty—none less inclined to take, or touch, aught which they have not honestly earned."

These laborers should beware attempts to deprive them of political rights like suffrage, a practice Lincoln said was common in the rebellious states. The reason is instructive: If they surrendered their political power, it would "surely be used to close the door of advancement against such as they, and to fix new disabilities and burdens upon them, till all of liberty shall be lost." Similarly, not only did rights drive progress, there was a right *to* progress. He said in Cincinnati: "This progress by which the poor, honest, industrious, and resolute man raises himself, that he may work on his own account, and hire somebody else, is that progress that human nature is entitled to, is that improvement in condition that is intended to be secured by those institutions under which we live, is the great principle for which this government was really formed."

Liberty and Prudence

Burke's and Lincoln's ideas of liberty are far from identical, but both are ample as well as grounded in what we have seen are the basic requirements of prudence. Each understood liberty in limited, definable terms rather than in the unbounded and intangible—and therefore unaccountable and illimitable—sense of the French Revolution. For Lincoln as for Burke, natural rights were universal in reach because they were limited in scope. For both, they were also achieved in concrete circumstances. Burke, for example, defended the rights of the American colonists as they descended from British tradition, while Lincoln used natural rights rhetoric to correct the profound wrong of slavery, not to achieve any utopian vision.

Both Burke and Lincoln tethered reason to the sentiments. Burke regarded feelings as a more reliable and more broadly recognized guide than disputable and often arrogant reason. Lincoln unquestionably gave more play to the abstract, but he also confined its application to situations in which it was unavoidable: slavery in territories that had no government. Lincoln's liberty was also more universal, as we have seen, than Burke's idea of inheritance, but the two were linked insofar as Lincoln's universals operated only by example and applied only to the most fundamental of rights—which Burke, too, had ascribed to nature.

As we shall now see, both Burke's and Lincoln's politics shared a final, crucial commonality: a reverence for custom that is well known in the former's thought and underappreciated in the latter's.

CHAPTER SEVEN

⟨⟩ ⟨⟩

The Collected Reason
of Ages

Burke and Lincoln on Custom

In his 1780 "Tract on the Popery Laws," a brief in favor of the religious rights of Irish Catholics, Burke satirized his opponents as employing the argument he had long been accused of using: Their "argument ad verecundiam has as much force as any such have," he wrote: in other words, as much authority as other logical fallacies. The Latin reference is to the "argument from authority," the fallacy according to which a conclusion is declared to be right solely because it accords with an authoritative source. In a 1780 parliamentary debate on reforming the royal court, Burke accused a defender of the crown of arguing similarly and declared he "would readily answer" it.

Yet the argument from authority that Burke denounces is the same one he is wrongly accused of using in his appeals to history and custom. Timothy Michael calls the argument from authority "the dominant mode in the *Reflections*," adding that it also plays a "more subordinate role in Burke's more nuanced writings on India, America, Ireland, and slavery...." But this is to misunderstand the nature of Burke's appeal to custom, which he believed reflected accumulated wisdom applied to circumstance. In Burke's famous description of "the science of jurisprudence" in the *Reflections*, custom—in this case the common law—contains

"the collected reason of ages, combining the principles of original justice
with the infinite variety of human concerns...." A Jacobin regime would
reject this study, and the reason is instructive: "Personal self-sufficiency
and arrogance (the certain attendants upon all those who have never
experienced a wisdom greater than their own) would usurp the tribunal."

The problem, in other words, was arrogance. Burke's suspicion of *individual* reason lay at the heart of his critique of the rejection of custom,
just as it lay beneath his critique of metaphysical politics. The argument
from authority was fallacious because it appealed to authority simply
as authority. But when Burke grounded arguments in custom, he invariably meant the *collected, historical* reason that custom reflected and
contained. The argument was never that the extant was always good. As
Levin observes, it is "that reform must proceed gradually for practical,
political, social, and moral reasons." In the Hastings trial, for example,
the defendant claimed that bribery was legitimate because it was a custom of Indian politics. Burke denied that corruption was ever a custom
of India, but more importantly, he declined to defend "vicious practices
and customs, which it is the business of good laws and good customs to
eradicate." Good laws alone would be insufficient. The laws must instruct
and improve the customs.

In this chapter, we shall engage Burke's rich understanding of custom
as a storehouse of wisdom, beginning with its clearest legal and theoretical
manifestation: prescription, the Roman law by which long possession
generated a right to property—and, on Burke's view, government. Then,
we shall turn to Lincoln's appeals to tradition, which differed but are not
wholly distinct from Burke's.

"The Solid Rock" of Prescription

Writing to his son Richard on Irish affairs in 1793, Burke explained that
"the solid rock" of prescription was the only reasonable means of creating
a title to property. It was

> the soundest, the most general, and the most recognized title between
> man and man that is known in municipal or in public jurisprudence...a
> title in which not arbitrary institutions, but the eternal order of things,
> gives judgment; a title which is not the creature, but the master, of

positive law; a title which, though not fixed in its term, is rooted in its principle in the law of Nature itself, and is indeed the original ground of all known property: for all property in soil will always be traced back to that source, and will rest there.

This use of "the law of Nature" to describe prescription implicitly rejects the Lockean theory of property, according to which an individual takes possession of a part of the commons by improving it. Locke's theory would lead to sudden jolts in ownership, and it was hostile to the stability of property required for a landed aristocracy. Burke sought a sturdier, steadier basis for property, one where, as he wrote in the passage above, it could "rest." Notice that other institutions would be "arbitrary." Prescription, by contrast, was "the original ground of all known property." In rejecting Locke, who sought to impose an abstract theory on property, Burke chose slow evolution over speculative politics. This was the only way property could be stabilized: "If prescription be once shaken," he urged in the *Reflections*, "no species of property is secure, when it once becomes an object large enough to tempt the cupidity of indigent power."

This, again, was ancient Roman law. Burke's innovation was to apply it to political life. One purpose of prescription was to conceal the ugly beginnings of many governments and reconcile people to them over time. He wrote in the *Reflections* that, had the French Revolution overthrown an actual tyranny, which Burke insisted it did not, prescription might eventually have legitimized it: "If they had set up this new, experimental government as a necessary substitute for an expelled tyranny, mankind would anticipate the time of prescription, which through long usage mellows into legality governments that were violent in their commencement."

Because the Revolution could not claim prescriptive authority, "the present rulers in our neighboring country, regenerated as they are...have no more right to the territory called France than I have," he wrote in the *Appeal*. Burke sarcastically inquired: "Who are they who claim by prescription and descent from certain gangs of banditti called Franks, and Burgundians, and Visigoths, of whom I may have never heard, and ninety-nine out of an hundred of themselves certainly never have heard, whilst at the very time they tell me that prescription and long possession form no title to property?"

Burke also used prescription to criticize British abuses. He told the sheriffs of Bristol that the American colonists had become used to having their own legislatures "by imperceptible habits, and old custom, the great support of all the governments in the world." Warren Hastings's installation of a tyrant in a region of India was unjustifiable because it was sudden and new. It "was a usurpation yet green in the country, and the country felt uneasy under it," Burke said in the impeachment trial. "It had not the advantage of that prescriptive usage, that inveterate habit, that traditionary opinion, which a long continuance of any system of government secures to it."

The British constitution was prescriptive in that its authority derived not from any theoretical purity but rather from its duration: The House of Commons, for example, was "a legislative body corporate by prescription, not made upon any given theory, but existing prescriptively,—just like the rest," he said in a 1782 debate on parliamentary representation. This rejection of theory as the basis for what was actually political custom did not mean Burke was appealing to authority. Far from it: He was appealing to the weakness of contemporary as opposed to enduring reason. "Nor is prescription of government formed upon blind, unmeaning prejudices," he explained in the 1782 debate. "For man is a most unwise and a most wise being. The individual is foolish; the multitude, for the moment, is foolish, when they act without deliberation; but the species is wise, and, when time is given to it, as a species, it almost always acts right."

For this reason, Burke wrote in the *Appeal* that those who were unable to admire "those writers or artists (Livy and Virgil, for instance, Raphael or Michael Angelo) whom all the learned had admired" should not "follow [their] own fancies" but should rather seek to grasp what they should assume eluded their understanding. This was "as good a rule, at least, with regard to [the British] Constitution. We ought to understand it according to our measure, and to venerate where we are not able presently to comprehend." Burke's emphasis on custom was closely related to his reasoning from circumstance. The "expedience" of a constitution was to be judged by its contribution to the public good, and in the case of an extant rather than a new regime, the proof could only lie in experience. "What has been found expedient or inexpedient?" Burke asked in the 1782 debate. "And I will not take [reformers'] *promise* rather than the performance of the Constitution."

It was a function of prescription, and prudence, to capture the wisdom of the species over time and convert it into habit: "Prescription is the most solid of all titles, not only to property, but, which is to secure that property, to government.... It is accompanied with another ground of authority in the constitution of the human mind, presumption. It is a presumption in favor of any settled scheme of government against any untried project, that a nation has long existed and flourished under it." Notice again that "authority" accrued to a government because it had worked well for a "long" period, another indication that Burke did not simply defer to the extant.

This "presumption" suggests another dimension of Burkean prudence descending from long use: "prejudice." Burke employed the word frequently and literally to connote judgment in advance. The function of prejudice was to secure deference from individual reason in the moment to the wisdom of the people over time. Jacobinism, by contrast, worked in reverse: Writing to William Smith in 1795 to urge the emancipation of Irish Catholics lest they turn in desperation to Jacobinism, Burke asked: "What is Jacobinism? It is an attempt (hitherto but too successful) to eradicate prejudice out of the minds of men, for the purpose of putting all power and all authority into the hands of the persons capable of occasionally enlightening the minds of the people." It is striking that the function of discrete, contemporary reason was the concentration of power, which prejudice dispersed over generations. This power sought "the destruction of all prejudices," Burke wrote in the *Appeal*, explaining that prejudices were, in turn, nearly identical with "moral sentiments." The reference to "sentiments" amid this critique of metaphysical politics is revealing. Moral sentiments were, in fact, all that the *Appeal* said could "put some check on [the *philosophes'*] savage theories," which were rationally illimitable. Prejudice was so central that a nation or people—a moral rather than a geographical concept, Burke wrote—would be destroyed without it.

All the "principal religions in Europe," Burke told Smith, were prescriptive: "They have all stood long enough to make prescription and its chain of legitimate prejudices their main stay." The suggestion was not that all prejudices were legitimate—a point he also made in his disassociation of prescription from "blind, unmeaning prejudices"—but rather that those that had "stood long enough" were likely to be. The reason, again, was not that the extant was always legitimate; it was that wisdom accumulated by the long application of principle to circumstances was likelier to be right. In his "Letter to a Noble Lord," Burke for this reason counterposed the wisdom of prescription to the folly of the Revolutionary *philosophes* of France: "The learned professors of the Rights of Man regard prescription not as a title to bar all claim set up against old possession, but they look on prescription as itself a bar against the possessor and proprietor. They hold an immemorial possession to be no more than a long continued and therefore an aggravated injustice." Arrogance about their own reasoning capacities had set the law of nature, prescription, on its head.

"Where I Can Neither Wander nor Stumble"

Prejudice was instantiated in custom. Burke's deference to it was, again, anchored in humility about individual reason. He said in his speech on conciliation with the colonies that he was determined not to propose measures based on his own judgment alone: "Above all things, I was resolved not to be guilty of tampering,—the odious vice of restless and unstable minds. I put my foot in the tracks of our forefathers, where I can neither wander nor stumble." This propensity to meddle with con- stitutional mechanisms was a "vice" that reflected an "unstable mind," whereas a virtuous and stable person would recognize the limits of his own reason. Burke recognized the vitality of mystery to religious and political life as early as his notebook in the 1750s, whose essay "Philoso- phy and Learning" declares: "Perhaps the bottom of most things is un- intelligible; and our surest reasoning, when we come to a certain point, is involved not only in obscurity but contradiction." As Bourke notes, Burke's attempt to preserve a realm for the mysterious was the operating principle of *A Vindication of Natural Society*. The attempt to render all things rational and susceptible of axiomatic proof corroded the ties of prejudice on which the British constitution—"the great contexture of this mysterious whole," Burke said in his speech on conciliation with the colonies—depended. He said in the Hastings trial that prescription relied on a sense of mystery about origins: "There is a sacred veil to be drawn over the beginnings of all governments. Ours in India had an origin like those which time has sanctified by obscurity. Time, in the origin of most governments, has thrown this mysterious veil over them;

prudence and discretion make it necessary to throw something of the same drapery over more recent foundations...."

This humility about reason applied within generations as well as across them. Burke wrote to the sheriffs of Bristol that he hoped they were not operating on the demonstrably inaccurate presumption that all political actors were equally corrupt, because such would elevate their individual judgment over that of the community acting over time: "A conscientious person would rather doubt his own judgment than condemn his species. He would say, 'I have observed without attention, or judged upon erroneous maxims; I trusted to profession, when I ought to have attended to conduct.' Such a man will grow wise, not malignant, by his acquaintance with the world."

The particular vice of the French Revolution was this kind of malignance, which manifested in a deliberate, antinomian rejection of custom simply because it was custom. He had warned Depont that France was about "to live in a new order of things; under a plan of Government of which no Man can speak from experience." The absence of experience alarmed Burke because experience was the only way something as complex as a political regime could be tested. But the rejection of the past was precisely what so attracted the Revolutionary French. The *Reflections* explained: "They have no respect for the wisdom of others; but they pay it off by a very full measure of confidence in their own. With them it is a sufficient motive to destroy an old scheme of things, because it is an old one. As to the new, they are in no sort of fear with regard to the duration of a building run up in haste; because duration is no object to those who think little or nothing has been done before their time, and who place all their hopes in discovery." Burke's disdain for Revolutionary arrogance was palpable. Their "whole principle is to despise the ancient, permanent sense of mankind, and to set up a scheme of society on new principles"; consequently, they "must naturally expect that such of us who think better of the judgment of the human race than of theirs, should consider both them and their devices as men and schemes upon their trial. They must take it for granted that we attend much to their reason, but not at all to their authority." The passage shows once more that Burke was not hostile to "reason," but "authority" accrued to it only when generations endorsed it. The reason of the species exceeded the reason of the individual.

The converse also held: A sudden formation of government based on theory was a perilous undertaking, an observation that provoked some of Burke's strongest language in the *Reflections*:

> The very idea of the fabrication of a new government is enough to fill us with disgust and horror. We wished at the period of the Revolution, and do now wish, to derive all we possess as *an inheritance from our fore-fathers*. Upon that body and stock of inheritance we have taken care not to inoculate any scion alien to the nature of the original plant. All the reformations we have hitherto made have proceeded upon the principle of reference to antiquity; and I hope, nay, I am persuaded, that all those which possibly may be made hereafter will be carefully formed upon analogical precedent, authority, and example.

This passage requires careful attention. As we shall see more fully presently, Burke regarded custom as an "inheritance" that was not to be corrupted by the addition of foreign elements but rather "reform[ed]" according to its original principles. Future changes would be made on the same basis, with precedents that could be analogized to the original principles, the authority of custom, and its examples. The British had always claimed liberties "as an entailed inheritance derived to us from our forefathers, and to be transmitted to our posterity,—as an estate specially belonging to the people of this kingdom, without any reference to any other more general or prior right."

The British constitution, Burke emphasized in the 1782 debate, was "a choice not of one day or one set of people, not a tumultuary and giddy choice; it is a deliberate election of ages and of generations; it is a constitution, made by what is ten thousand times better than choice; it is made by the peculiar circumstances, occasions, tempers, dispositions, and moral, civil, and social habitudes of the people, which disclose themselves only in a long space of time." This gradual development, as opposed to a discrete moment of conception and consent, enabled the regime to accommodate itself to the specific needs of a particular people. A regime could not discover or adapt to circumstances in a single moment of founding; only one that evolved gradually could. The British constitution, the *Appeal* consequently explained, had "not been struck out at an heat by a set of presumptuous men, like the Assembly of pettifoggers run mad in

Paris." In the same text, he viciously satirized the French constitution by reference to the Roman tradition that Minerva, the goddess of wisdom, had entered the world fully armed directly from the brain of her father, Jupiter: "What! alter our sublime Constitution, the glory of France, the envy of the world, the pattern for mankind, the masterpiece of legislation, the collected and concentrated glory of this enlightened age? Have we not produced it ready-made and ready-armed, mature in its birth, a perfect goddess of wisdom and of war, hammered by our blacksmith midwives out of the brain of Jupiter himself?"

"An Entailed Inheritance"

Burke's notion of entail, the law according to which inherited land had to be transmitted through generations intact, suggests that a people does not have the authority to lay waste to custom. The metaphor of inheritance was important to Burke because it ennobled freedom by providing a principle of restraint in the form of respect for one's ancestors and duty to one's descendants. He wrote in the *Reflections*: "Always acting as if in the presence of canonized forefathers, the spirit of freedom, leading in itself to misrule and excess, is tempered with an awful gravity. This idea of a liberal descent inspires us with a sense of habitual native dignity, which prevents that upstart insolence almost inevitably adhering to and disgracing those who are the first acquirers of any distinction. By this means our liberty becomes a noble freedom."

As early as the 1769 Whig pamphlet we encountered above, Burke had bemoaned that his opponents had "no reverence for the customs of our ancestors" and, significantly—the direct alternative to custom—"no attachment but to private interest, nor any zeal but for selfish gratifications." The "Tract on the Popery Laws" similarly said that Irish Catholics should not be punished "for acting upon a principle which of all others is perhaps the most necessary for preserving society, an implicit admiration and adherence to the establishments of their forefathers." He continued: "If we must resort to prepossessions for the ground of opinion, it is in the nature of man rather to defer to the wisdom of times past, whose weakness is not before his eyes, than to the present, of whose imbecility he has daily experience. Veneration of antiquity is congenial to the human mind."

It was no special trick to undermine generational institutions, the *Reflections* said, because "[t]he errors and defects of old establishments are visible and palpable." What was particularly dangerous was the combination of "absolute power" with this hostility to custom. The two fed on one another: As custom eroded, tyranny mounted. The Revolutionary French "teach the people to abhor and reject all feodality as the barbarism of tyranny; and they tell them afterwards how much of that barbarous tyranny they are to bear with patience." In such a circumstance, "it requires but a word" to sweep both good and bad away in a reflexive spasm of reform. "To make everything the reverse of what they have seen is quite as easy as to destroy.... At once to preserve and to reform is quite another thing." A reverence for custom, by contrast, led to prudent, gradual reform in which problems could be identified and addressed as they arose:

> By a slow, but well-sustained progress, the effect of each step is watched; the good or ill success of the first gives light to us in the second; and so, from light to light, we are conducted with safety through the whole series. We see that the parts of the system do not clash. The evils latent in the most promising contrivances are provided for as they arise. One advantage is as little as possible sacrificed to another. We compensate, we reconcile, we balance. We are enabled to unite into a consistent whole the various anomalies and contending principles that are found in the minds and affairs of men. From hence arises, not an excellence in simplicity, but one far superior, an excellence in composition.

We recall in this context that the prudent mind was "enlarged" and possessed of a faculty for "combining," as well as Burke's observation that while intricate schemes of policy were dangerous, constitutional complexity was essential because it enabled a unity of "anomalies" that arose not just in human minds but in human "affairs." Notice the essential role of experience in prudent judgment: "The means taught by experience may be better suited to political ends than those contrived in the original project." This could have been uttered by Aquinas, for whom ends were fixed while judgment as to means was the realm of prudence.

One result of this respect for custom was to ensure that change occurred at a deliberate and therefore prudent pace. The *Reflections* called it a "settled maxim" that the British had determined "never entirely nor at once to depart from antiquity." The *Appeal* said that Burke utilized "what the ancients call *mos majorum*"—the unwritten code of Roman traditions—as a guide for judgment because it enabled safe speculation. "That point being fixed, and laying fast hold of a strong bottom, our speculations may swing in all directions without public detriment, because they will ride with secure anchorage."

This was also why one should not draw gratuitous attention to flaws in an ancient constitution. Exposing defects in administration was one thing, but "a declaration of defects, real or supposed, in the fundamental constitution of your country" was dangerous, Burke said in the 1782 reform debate. The *Reflections* went further. Gratuitous change was worse than reflexive conservation:

> To avoid, therefore, the evils of inconstancy and versatility, ten thousand times worse than those of obstinacy and the blindest prejudice, we have consecrated the state, that no man should approach to look into its defects or corruptions but with due caution; that he should never dream of beginning its reformation by its subversion; that he should approach to the faults of the state as to the wounds of a father, with pious awe and trembling solicitude.

This piety was also how Lincoln approached the founding fathers.

"The Mystic Chords of Memory": Lincoln on Custom

Lincoln is often thought, as by Weaver, to reason from universally applicable principles. There is something to that, as we have seen, but for him those principles were also inseparable from the American political tradition in which he found them. We have already seen him appeal to the sacrifices of the founding fathers in the Lyceum Address. This turn to tradition was a staple of Lincoln's political rhetoric from the beginning. Speaking on the Sub-Treasury Plan in 1839, for example, Lincoln underscored the constitutionality of a national bank by reference to its support among "a majority of the Revolutionary patriarchs, whoever acted officially on the question, commencing with Gen. Washington and embracing Gen. Jackson, the larger number of signers of the Declaration, and of the framers of the Constitution, who were in the Congress of 1791...."

As typified him, Lincoln's clearest appeals to tradition—"the good old 'central ideas' of the Republic," he said at a Chicago Republican banquet in 1856—came in response to slavery. The Declaration of Independence played a special role in these appeals, where it blended in Lincoln's soul with both reason and memory. "I have never had a feeling politically that did not spring from the sentiments embodied in the Declaration of Independence," he said at Independence Hall on his journey to his 1861 inauguration. Lincoln, of course, appealed to something that was intrinsically right about the Declaration, but also to the shared inheritance of it. Immediately after the statement just quoted, Lincoln continued: "I have often pondered over the dangers which were incurred by the men who assembled here and adopted that Declaration of Independence—I have pondered over the toils that were endured by the officers and soldiers of the army, who achieved that Independence." They toiled, significantly, for a "great principle or idea…something in that Declaration giving liberty, not alone to the people of this country, but hope to the world for all future time." This is, again, more universal than the particularistic idiom in which Burke spoke, as in his reference to liberties as "an entailed inheritance" of the British people. But Lincoln was not satisfied simply to invoke the Declaration's rightness. He also called forth the shared memories that bound the nation arising from it.

In a speech in Chicago just after the Fourth of July in 1858, Lincoln turned to the principles of the Declaration as the cause of the nation's prosperity. Importantly, Americans then could not trace ties of blood to the founding period, "but when they look through that old Declaration of Independence they find that those old men say that 'We hold these truths to be self-evident, that all men are created equal,' and then they feel that that moral sentiment taught in that day evidences their relation to those men, that it is the father of all moral principle in them, and that they have a right to claim it as though they were blood of the blood, and flesh of the flesh of the men who wrote that Declaration…." This is, again, a combination of custom and reason: The rightness of the principle creates the grounds for customary invocations of it. It is once more different from Burke, but not fundamentally so: We might say that whereas Lincoln discovered custom in principle, Burke found principle contained in the accumulated wisdom of custom. But even if from opposite directions, both men fused the two. In either case, repeated appeals were made to custom. Lincoln in fact nearly echoed Burke's notion of reforming in order to restore when he told the New Jersey Senate in February 1861 that he was "exceedingly anxious that this Union, the Constitution, and the liberties of the people shall be perpetuated in accordance with the *original idea* for which that struggle was made…" (emphasis added).

Lincoln likewise often appealed to the nation's great statesmen as authorities who enhanced, though they did not substitute for, the argument he was making. In an August 1858 draft of a speech, he invoked Thomas Jefferson and Andrew Jackson for his argument that Supreme Court decisions were not imbued with "binding political authority." In the Lincoln-Douglas debate at Ottawa, Illinois, he quoted Henry Clay, who "once said of a class of men who would repress all tendencies to liberty and ultimate emancipation, that they must, if they would do this, go back to the era of our Independence, and muzzle the cannon which thunders its annual joyous return…."

The meaning of the Declaration was a major ground of Lincoln's dispute with Douglas, who joined pro-slavery Southerners and the *Dred Scott* opinion in explicitly excluding African Americans from its promise of equality. Here again, he felt the founders merited deference. He said in the Lincoln-Douglas debate at Galesburg, Illinois: "[I] believe the entire records of the world, from the date of the Declaration of Independence up to within three years ago, may be searched in vain for one single affirmation, from one single man, that the negro was not included in the Declaration of Independence. I think I may defy Judge Douglas to show that he ever said so, that Washington ever said so, that any President ever said so, that any member of Congress ever said so…." Jefferson, he acknowledged, owned slaves but also said he "trembled for his country when he remembered that God was just…." Lincoln wrote in an 1859 letter that he was working "to save the principles of Jefferson from total overthrow in this nation."

Lincoln's most evocative reference to the Declaration and the nation's shared past was the Gettysburg Address, which opens with a reference to history, not to the abstract truths of the Declaration: "Four score and seven years ago our fathers brought forth on this continent, a new nation, conceived in Liberty, and dedicated to the proposition that all men are created equal." The important point is that Lincoln did not merely turn to the abstract truth of that proposition. He first anchored it in history. Earlier that year, in July 1863, Lincoln waxed rhapsodic in response to a serenade at the White House, describing the nation's extraordinary shared memory that the only two signers of the Declaration to become presidents both died on the document's 50th anniversary.

A common interpretation of Lincoln holds that he rescued the Declaration's ideal of equality from the Constitution's accommodation of slavery. A converse of that argument, that Lincoln "derailed" a tradition that had not theretofore emphasized equality, has been offered by Willmoore Kendall and George W. Carey. But there is no record that Lincoln ever saw a conflict between the Declaration and the Constitution. A draft speech in 1857 gave thanks to "our good old constitution" that disputes could be resolved with ballots rather than bullets. Lincoln was so devoted to the Constitution as fundamental law that he was willing to swallow the exceedingly bitter pill of its fugitive slave clause to maintain the Union.

His masterwork of historical analysis and evidentiary synthesis in this regard was the 1860 Cooper Union Address, which vaulted Lincoln into consideration for the Republican nomination through a conclusive demonstration that most of the framers of the Constitution opposed the expansion of slavery. In assessing Lincoln's fidelity to tradition, we are less concerned with the details of that analysis than with why he undertook it. The most immediate reason was to refute Douglas's suggestion that the founding fathers were moral agnostics on the question of slavery who surrendered the issue to local decision. But there is a deeper moral claim about the authority of custom that bears careful attention and comparison with Burke:

> Now, and here, let me guard a little against being misunderstood. I do not mean to say we are bound to follow implicitly in whatever our fathers did. To do so, would be to discard all the lights of current experience—to reject all progress—all improvement. What I do say is, that if we would supplant the opinions and policy of our fathers in any case, we should do so upon evidence so conclusive, and argument so clear, that even their great authority, fairly considered and weighed, cannot stand; and most surely not in a case whereof we ourselves declare they understood the question better than we.

This is different from Burke's attitude toward custom, which regarded it as more authoritative and thus engaged in reform to restore original principles. Lincoln was open to progress beyond founding principles if those were demonstrated to be errant. But the passage is also notable for what Burke called "presumption": namely, a presumption in favor of the founding fathers and a burden of proof for those who would overturn their work. Such was the basis of Lincoln's appeal to the "great authority" of the founders, which served the cause of prudence by supplying a high standard against which to judge our own reason. He appealed to the South on these grounds. Southerners claimed to be conservatives, he noted, asking what conservatism meant. "Is it not adherence to the old and tried, against the new and untried? We stick to, contend for, the identical old policy on the point in controversy which was adopted by 'our fathers who framed the Government under which we live;' while you with one accord reject, and scout, and spit upon that old policy, and insist upon substituting something new." He continued: "It was not we, but you, who discarded the old policy of the fathers."

Lincoln saw the Declaration and the Constitution as wholly compatible. As we have seen, the Constitution anticipated and enabled progress on the issue of slavery in accord with the values of the Declaration. Still, there is no question that the Declaration played an essential role in Lincoln's political thought. The Declaration was, he wrote in his January 1861 "Fragment on Constitution and Union," the Book of Proverbs' "apple of gold" contained in the Constitution's "picture of silver." The values of the Declaration, that is, formed the foundation for the Constitution. "The picture was made, not to *conceal*, or *destroy* the apple; but to *adorn*, and *preserve* it. The *picture* was made *for* the apple—*not* the apple for the picture." This was to say that the Declaration was morally prior to the Constitution, but the two worked in tandem and compatibility, as evidenced in Lincoln's exhortation to "act, that neither *picture*, or *apple* shall ever be blurred, or bruised or broken." The "neither" indicates he saw no contradiction in preserving both.

Earlier, speaking in Kalamazoo, Michigan, in 1856, he had likewise urged his "Democratic friends" to "[t]hrow off these things, and come to the rescue of this great principle of equality. Don't interfere with anything in the Constitution. That must be maintained, for it is the only safeguard of our liberties." Again, the distinction with Burke is nuanced but unmistakable. The Constitution—which, we observe, should not be interfered with even as we "rescue" the Declaration's "principle of equality," again suggesting the two are compatible—should be maintained because it serves a purpose. But for Burke, too, the appeal to custom was not merely an argument from simple authority but rather a recognition that the old was likelier to meet the criterion of wisdom and utility.

The lyrical peroration of Lincoln's First Inaugural supplies what may be an even clearer example of an appeal to custom in the form of shared history. Earlier in the speech, he had referred to historical authority in arguing that the Union was formed prior to the Declaration and continued by it. "The mystic chords of memory, stretching from every battle-field, and patriot grave, to every living heart and hearthstone, all over this broad land, will yet swell the chorus of the Union, when again touched, as surely they will be, by the better angels of our nature." Union should be maintained not merely on the basis of sober legal argument—which Lincoln had offered up to that point in the address—but rather on the foundation of common memories that created shared affections. At Gettysburg, he sought to place the fallen soldiers of that battle in the pantheon of heroes whose memories would bind future generations: "But, in a larger sense, we can not dedicate—we can not consecrate—we can not hallow—this ground. The brave men, living and dead, who struggled here, have consecrated it, far above our poor power to add or detract. The world will little note, nor long remember what we say here, but it can never forget what they did here. It is for us the living, rather, to be dedicated here to the unfinished work which they who fought here have thus far so nobly advanced." These dead should inspire Americans to complete the task before them, just as he had turned 25 years before to the example of the Revolution in the Lyceum Address.

Custom and Prudence

How are custom and prudence linked? Custom, like circumstance, is a principle of limitation, moderation, and gradualism. Lincoln, for instance, most certainly found slavery to be an abstract wrong but was inhibited from pursuing its abolition rashly by the forms of the Constitution he inherited. Yet those forms, especially the Declaration, were also essential for setting the proper ends of political life. In this sense, we may say that the "apple of gold"—the Declaration—supplied an immovable end, while the Constitution's "picture of silver" required prudential choices as to the means of attainment. For Burke, as we have seen, custom was a storehouse of wisdom that hemmed the otherwise illimitable operation of individual reason.

Yet this raises a difficult question. In an age of instant communication and, more important, instant political gratification—when common memory not only has grown distant but is in many cases actively desecrated—what space is left for prudence? In a time of hardening polarization that escalates the stakes not just of every election but also of every individual issue, have we lost the capacity—so essential to prudence—of telling the difference between genuine emergency and ordinary times? Can this ethic of prudence be restored? The conclusion to this study will explore these and other questions.

CONCLUSION

ℬ ℭ

Liberty and Authority, Patience and Resolve

Recovering the Politics of Prudence

In the Introduction to this study, we encountered Winston Churchill as a model of prudence whose statesmanship was calibrated to the ultimate circumstances he faced in the Nazi menace. Churchill was also well acquainted with both Burke and Lincoln. In his seminal essay "Consistency in Politics," Churchill wrote that Burke's writings on party and America "form the main and lasting armoury of Liberal opinion throughout the English-speaking world," while his writings on revolutionary France "will continue to furnish Conservatives for all time with the most formidable array of opposing weapons." And yet:

> No one can read the Burke of Liberty and the Burke of Authority without feeling that here was the same man pursuing the same ends, seeking the same ideals of society and Government, and defending them from assaults, now from one extreme, now from the other. The same danger approached the same man from different directions and in different forms, and the same man turned to face it with incomparable weapons, drawn from the same armoury, used in a different quarter, but for the same purpose.

This understanding of Burke also helps us to grasp both the full dimensions and the contemporary relevance of political prudence, as does Churchill's treatment of Lincoln in *The Great Democracies*, the fourth volume of his monumental *A History of the English-Speaking Peoples*. Churchill offered no summary sketch of Lincoln, but nonetheless supplied perceptive and illuminating remarks during the course of his narrative. Churchill wrote of the dissensions tearing at the nation over slavery in the late 1850s and in 1860: "Against this, Abraham Lincoln, in New York and elsewhere, unfolded in magnificent orations, calm, massive, and magnanimous, the anti-slavery cause." Lincoln's First Inaugural counseled "patience and conciliation," while he met the attack on Fort Sumter with "vehement resolve." Lincoln benefited from his enemies' relentless underestimation of him: "Lincoln's political foes, gazing upon him, did not know vigour when they saw it."

The prudent mind can exhibit all these qualities—liberty and authority, calmness and magnanimity, patience and resolve—at once. The key is knowing which to use at which moments. That is a faculty of judgment that not everyone possesses to the same extent: Certainly few are as able to perceive danger and counsel calm as Edmund Burke and Abraham Lincoln. But from their examples, some lessons are evident. One is that we should beware the rhetoric, increasingly emanating from all quarters of political dispute, of ultimate stakes in all affairs. To borrow a Burkean image we have already encountered, this "distemper...relaxes and wears out, by a vulgar and prostituted use, the spring of that spirit which is to be exerted only on great occasions."

If all issues are world-historical, none are; to declare all issues ultimate is to blind ourselves to those that actually are. Lincoln is justly remembered for what he did in perilous moments, but his prudent greatness consisted equally in his early perception—like Burke's attempt to conciliate the American colonies—that grave conflict was approaching and that it should be defused before it reached a breaking point. Lincoln yielded this hope only when Confederate guns fired on Fort Sumter; even afterwards, he considered gradual emancipation in border states that remained with the Union.

It would not be too much to say that for both men, moderation was a default position. It is not for us. Burke's prediction that "[m]oderation will be stigmatized as the virtue of cowards, and compromise as the prudence of traitors" has proven substantially correct. Times vary, of course, and moments of great divides come and go. But something has changed. The acceleration of contact between us, and the myriad ways in which technology enables each person to isolate himself from divergent views, is making it easier to see others as enemies and moderates as cowards and traitors. To endorse moderation is not to say prudence is a geographic or geometric virtue that automatically lies between whatever the shifting political extremes might be. It is rather to endorse moderation in one's own thought, moderation in one's own confidence, moderation in one's own position, wherever on the spectrum it may fall. In his *The Roots of American Order*, Russell Kirk grasped this feature of Lincoln's moderation:

> Lincoln was a man of order, not a man of theoretic dogmas in politics. Having risen from very low estate, he knew the savagery that lies close beneath the skin of man, and he saw that most men are law-abiding only out of obedience to routine and custom and convention. The self-righteous Abolitionist and the reckless Fire-eater were abhorrent to him; yet he took the middle path between them not out of any misapplication of Aristotle's doctrine of the golden mean, but because he held that the unity and security of the United States transcended any fanatic scheme of perfectibility. In his immediate object, the preserving of the Union, he succeeded through the ancient virtue of *prudentia*.

All this is inseparable from the importance of calibrating action to circumstance. As Lincoln teaches in the Lyceum Address, some times require greatness while others call for prudent moderation. The statesman faces an inherent conflict of interest in this judgment, for the magnitude of his historical image hinges—such are the vagaries of how history is written—on the perceived magnitude of his times. Statesmen who seek a place in the rolls of greatness have little incentive for prudence. The Lyceum Address was, in this sense, an attempt at chastening ambition.

If we wish to do so as well, we might also reconsider how we reward political action. Historical reviews of great statesmen almost never account for whether their statesmanship was calibrated to their times: The assumption is that greatness finds its place in achieving change. But this measure, which assumes change is always warranted and necessarily good, has no place for prudence. The statesman who averts great danger and the one who confronts it may be equally prudent depending on the circumstances each faces; so may be the one who achieves change and the one who inhibits or does not seek it. We should celebrate the Burke of conciliation alike with the Burke of resistance; the Lincoln of compromise alongside the Lincoln of bold resolve.

This modification of civic standards is one answer to a question with which my late teacher George W. Carey, a Burkean, once vexed me. The query still perplexes. How does one teach prudence? Surely one need not invest prudence with mystical qualities to see that some people have innate capacities for judgment and perception that others do not—capacities that cannot be taught or transferred from one to another. Aristotle associates prudence with "perception" arising from "intellect," and "a person is held to have judgment, comprehension, and intellect by nature"—not, that is, by training. Yet this innate capacity must be sharpened by experience. Aristotle continues: "[O]ne ought to pay attention to the undemonstrated assertions and opinions of experienced and older people, or of the prudent, no less than to demonstrations, for because they have an experienced eye, they see correctly."

Yet even if we cannot always instill the capacity for prudence, we can teach its elements. We can show it by example through genuine instruction in the unapologetic histories of great and prudent statesmanship. Most important, we can send a strong civic signal by honoring this vital, binding dimension of politics rather than dismissing all forms of caution and moderation as "false, reptile prudence." Our rush to do so reflects an incapacity for the subtle judgment—perhaps for subtlety itself—that prudence demands. Prudence above all else is not just able but willing to make distinctions, something against which the contemporary mind—always aching for a scientistic rule to replace judgment and the responsibility judgment entails—rebels.

This yearning for rules helps to explain the modern emphasis on what Mary Ann Glendon, in her unsurpassed 1991 book of the same name, has called *Rights Talk*. We can associate such talk with Burke and Lincoln only by slicing quotations from context and, more important, from the broader corpus of their work. Neither excerpted rights from the broader context of political community or from the superintending standards of limitation and the public good. Their standards of what was natural and nonnegotiable were so basic as to present themselves equally to both the sentiments and the reason. Rights were not a substitute for either judgment or politics. Burke in particular recognized the propensity of rootless rights talk to fly into fanaticisms, but for both men, invocations of rights were rooted in prudence. They should be for us.

To relax these claims of rights, we must reclaim what may be the most important dimension of prudence: what Burke called "a moral rather than a complexional timidity." Judge Learned Hand famously described liberty as "the spirit which is not too sure that it is right...." It is not *too* sure: It is appropriately confident and resolute, but not inordinately so. Lincoln's growing invocations of grace during the Civil War were evidence that his humility deepened even as his greatness rose. Burke, meanwhile, theorized humility without fetishizing it. He made it a virtue of the strong and the resolved. His suspicion of the lone individual's reason against the aggregate of the species projected over time and captured in custom was fundamentally an expression of the kind of humility he meant.

Perhaps above all, this is the prudence we have lost. This is an age of consummate faith not just in reason—which Burke certainly venerated in its proper place—but in a desiccated, technocratic rationality that deprives political life of meaning in search, rather, for objectively right answers to override the fallibility that is an indispensable part of our shared humanity. Our supreme self-confidence admits no prudence. It does not see unanticipated consequences, nor does it practice such virtues as moral timidity. Instead, it seeks a desolate world of cold reason and unbending rules, of dehumanized politics and lonely people. Here, there is no room for judgment, political life, or human responsibility. Prudence, restored to its throne as "the god of this lower world"—the prudence of Burke's liberty and authority, of Lincoln's patience and resolve—makes for a far lovelier and more livable place.

Notes on Sources

In order to keep this work accessible to the reader, I have opted not to encumber it with footnotes, instead endeavoring to identify especially primary sources within the body of the text. For Burke's writings, correspondence, and speeches, I have relied on the 12-volume *Works of the Right Honourable Edmund Burke*, available in facsimile from several publishers; the 10-volume *Correspondence of Edmund Burke* published by Cambridge University, Press, 1978; H. V. F. Somerset's *A Note-Book of Edmund Burke* (Cambridge University Press, 2011); and, for some writings not published in the *Works*, Jesse Norman's 2015 Everyman's Library edition of *Reflections on the Revolution in France and Other Writings*. For Lincoln, I have relied on Roy Basler's nine-volume *Collected Works of Abraham Lincoln* (Rutgers University Press, 1953). Readers interested in more compact selections for both thinkers will benefit from, for Burke, Liberty Fund's four-volume *Select Works of Edmund Burke*, Harvey C. Mansfield's *Selected Letters of Edmund Burke* (University of Chicago Press, 1984), and David Bromwich's *On Empire, Liberty, and Reform: Speeches and Letters* (Yale University Press, 2000); and, for Lincoln, Basler's *Abraham Lincoln: His Speeches and Writings* (Da Capo Press, 1990) and the Library of America two-volume set published in 1990 and edited by Don E. Fehrenbacher. I am indebted in particular to Mansfield's *Selected Letters*, whose introduction contains passages from which I have quoted and whose guide to the correspondence was an immense substantive help, and to the Library of America edition of Lincoln.

It is easy, and delightful, to get lost in these volumes, but the reader may find a broad sketch of a road map helpful. As a general guide, on the topic of prudence, Burke is never better than in his speeches on America, located in Volume 2 of the *Works*, and the *Reflections*, contained in Volume 3. These make an especially useful pairing because they show what Churchill called the "Burke of Liberty and the Burke of Authority" in his full, and consistent, dimensions. For the bold aspect of Burkean prudence, he is at his best in Volume 5's *Letters on a Regicide Peace*, in which attempts to appease the French directly aroused his ire, not merely because they were morally vacuous but also because they were imprudent. Burke discusses the issue of abstract reason, as well as revelation, throughout his writings. The *Reflections* are matchless in their discussion of untethered reason, as is his letter to Depont, located in Volume 6 of the *Correspondence*. His *Note-Book* contains several suggestive entries touching on these topics, including "Religion of No efficacy considered as a State Engine," "Religion," and "Several Scattered Hints concerning Philosophy and Learning." *Regicide Peace* explores the inherent and political atheism of the Jacobin regime. His speech in response to a petition from the Unitarian Society, in Volume 7 of the *Works*, explores both the limits of toleration and the importance of binding reason to circumstance.

On the topic of rights, Burke's letters to the Irish statesman Sir Hercule Langrishe and to his son Richard Burke, both in Volume 6 of the *Works*, are eloquent arguments for the fullest toleration for Irish Catholics. Volumes 8 through 12 concern the impeachment of Warren Hastings, the former governor-general of India; of these, Volumes 8 and 9 are mostly reports and charges, while Burke's eloquent opening speech is found in Volume 10, and Burke's speeches in reply to Hastings's defense are in Volumes 11 and 12. Volume 2's 1783 speech on Fox's East India Bill serves, meanwhile, as a compelling reminder that these were lifelong commitments for Burke. (The title of Chapter 5—"The Little Catechism of the Rights of Man"—comes from *Thoughts on French Affairs*, located in Volume 4.) On the topic of custom, the definitive work is again the *Reflections*, although Volume 1's *Vindication of Natural Society*, which must be read as satire, is also a revealing deconstruction of the kind of social-contract theorizing that would later lead the likes of Thomas Paine to believe the world could be forever made anew. Volume 4's *An Appeal from the New to the Old Whigs* roots Burke's view of the French Revolution in the customary position of the Whig Party in England. Needless to say, for a thinker of Burke's complexity, none of these topics is neatly separable from the others.

The same is true, but more so, for Lincoln—more so because his views must be gleaned and assembled from letters and speeches rather than full-scale tracts of the sort Burke wrote. It is impossible to divide these by topic because each text covers so many. The letters to the *Sangamo Journal* of his early campaigns are in Volume 1. So are the "Lyceum Address," an early elucidation of Lincolnian prudence, and the Temperance Address. The eulogies for Zachary Taylor and Henry Clay, as well as the Peoria Address, are in Volume 2. The Lincoln-Douglas debates and the Cooper Union speech are contained in Volume 3. The addresses Lincoln made on his way to his 1861 inauguration are in Volume 4, as is the First Inaugural and the first war message to Congress. From there, state papers and especially war correspondence consume most of the remaining volumes. The letter to General Joseph Hooker used as an epigraph above and assessed in Chapter 2 of this study is contained in Volume 6. The Gettysburg Address is in Volume 6, the Second Inaugural in Volume 8.

For selections from Aristotle, I have used Robert Bartlett and Susan Collins's edition of *The Nicomachean Ethics* (University of Chicago Press, 2011). Aristotle's most direct discussion of prudence is in Book 6, Chapter 5. The selections from Aquinas, including the epigraph, appear in *Nature and Grace: Selections from the Summa Theologica of Thomas Aquinas*, translated by A. M. Fairweather (Catholic Way Publishing, 2013). He discusses the relationship between providence and prudence in Question 22. For Tocqueville's *The Old Regime and the French Revolution*, see the Stuart Gilbert translation (Anchor Books, 1983), and for his 1852 address to the Academy of Arts and Sciences, see *Recollections: The French Revolution of 1848 and its Aftermath*, edited by Olivier Zunz and translated by Arthur Goldhammer (University of Virginia Press, 2016). I have consulted several sources in Churchill, including his *The Gathering Storm*, the first volume of his monumental history and memoir *The Second World War*, as well as *The Great Democracies*, the fourth volume of his *History of the English-Speaking Peoples*, both available from multiple publishers. The long quotation about Burke in the Conclusion comes from Churchill's essay "Consistency and Politics" in the delightfully wide-ranging collection of essays *Thoughts and Adventures: Churchill Reflects on Spies, Cartoons, Flying, and the Future*, edited by James W. Muller (Intercollegiate Studies Institute, 2009).

The literature on Burke and Lincoln is, one hardly need say, vast, and this book does not attempt a typical academic review of it. Perhaps the most comprehensive biography of Burke is F. P. Lock's two-volume work *Edmund Burke* (Oxford, 1999 and 2006). Among single-volume biographies, the definitive, if flawed, is arguably Conor Cruise O'Brien's *The Great Melody: A Thematic Biography of Edmund Burke* (University of Chicago Press, 1994), which offers the reader the benefit of taking Burke's ideas seriously but also distracts from them with its occasional drifts into psychological analysis. Other excellent short biographies include Russell Kirk's *Edmund Burke: A Genius Reconsidered* (Intercollegiate Studies Institute, 2009)—which, along with his *The Conservative Mind: From Burke To Eliot* (Gateway Editions, 2001), helped reclaim Burke for conservatism over the emphasis on his reforming side that had taken precedence in much of the previous literature—and Jesse Norman's recent *Edmund Burke: The First Conservative* (Basic Books, 2015), which blends biography with an assessment of the contemporary relevance of Burke's ideas.

Several intellectual biographies of Burke have recently appeared. David Bromwich's *The Intellectual Life of Edmund Burke: From the Sublime and Beautiful to American Independence* (Harvard University Press, 2014), which assesses the first half of Burke's career as part of a planned two-volume study, is a reminder that Burke supplies resources for all sides of political debate. Richard Bourke's *Empire & Revolution: The Political Life of Edmund Burke* (Princeton University Press, 2015) is a masterful assessment of Burke's ideas, replete with both penetrating analyses and creative selections from his readings. Quotes from these authors are from these works.

There is no shortage of works assessing Burke's political thought. Mansfield's *Statesmanship and Party Government: A Study of Burke and Bolingbroke* (University of Chicago Press, 2013) appraises Burke's views on statesmanship. Mansfield's unsurpassed overview of Burke in the third edition of Leo Strauss and Joseph Cropsey's *History of Political Philosophy* (University of Chicago Press, 1986) is, along with *Statesmanship and Party Government*, simultaneously among the closest but also most capacious readings of Burke. I have referred above to several of the interpretations of Burke that emphasize his affinity for the natural law. These include Kirk, Francis Canavan's *The Political Reason of Edmund Burke* (Duke University Press, 1960), Burleigh T. Wilkins's *The Problem of Burke's Political Philosophy* (Clarendon Press, 1967), and Peter J. Stanlis's *Edmund Burke & The Natural Law* (Transaction Publishers, 2015). Joseph Pappin III's *The Metaphysics of Edmund Burke* similarly casts Burke as a Thomist. More recently, Yuval Levin's *The Great Debate: Edmund Burke, Thomas Paine, and the Birth of Right and Left* (Basic Books, 2013), from which I have quoted throughout, makes its author's Burkean sympathies clear enough to the careful reader, but nonetheless provides an exceedingly equitable treatment of both thinkers.

There are also exceptional collections of essays on Burke, including Daniel E. Ritchie's *Edmund Burke: Appraisals and Appreciations* (Transaction, 1990), which encompasses major historical assessments of Burke by figures ranging from Walter Bagehot to Irving Babbitt (Babbitt's "Burke and the Moral Imagination," excerpted from his *Democracy and Leadership*, is the source of the quotation about the moral imagination in Chapter 3 above); Ian Crowe's *The Enduring Edmund Burke: Bicentennial Essays* (Intercollegiate Studies Institute, 1997), from which the quotation from Pappin in Chapter 5 is taken; and an electronic edition of *The University Bookman on Edmund Burke* (The Russell Kirk Center for Cultural Renewal, 2015). Crowe's *An Imaginative Whig: Reassessing the Life and Thought of Edmund Burke* (University of Missouri Press, 2005) is another outstanding collection, and his introductory essay to it is the source of the quotation about Burke's "historical imagination" in Chapter 3 above. There are several perceptive essays on Burke in *A Moral Enterprise: Politics, Reason, and the Human Good: Essays in Honor of Francis Canavan*, edited by Kenneth L. Grasso and Robert P. Hunt (Intercollegiate Studies Institute, 2002).

The first major biography of Lincoln was his law partner William Herndon's both celebrated and criticized *Life of Lincoln*. Needless to say, such volumes have continued to pour forth. The best recent ones include David Herbert Donald's *Lincoln* (Simon and Schuster, 1996) and Ronald White's *A. Lincoln* (Random House, 2009). The definitive authority on Lincoln's political thought is Harry V. Jaffa, whose *Crisis of the House Divided: An Interpretation of the Issues in the Lincoln-Douglas Debates* (University of Chicago Press, 2009) stands as the most careful reading of the statesman yet undertaken. The historian Allen C. Guelzo's contribution to understanding Lincoln's thought has been immeasurable, including but hardly limited to his *Abraham Lincoln as a Man of Ideas* (Southern Illinois University Press, 2009). Lewis Lehrman's *Lincoln at Peoria: The Turning Point* (Stackpole Books, 2008) is the best reading of perhaps the pivotal moment in Lincoln's political career. More recently, Lehrman's *Lincoln and Churchill: Statesmen at War* (Stackpole Books, 2018) has provided an

illuminating comparison of two prudent statesmen compelled to undertake bold measures in moments of existential national crisis.

David Lowenthal's *The Mind and Art of Abraham Lincoln, Philosopher
Statesman: Texts and Interpretations of Twenty Great Speeches* (Lexington
Books, 2012) provides close interpretations of often neglected Lincolnian
texts, even if Lowenthal is sometimes too quick to dismiss Lincoln's
unorthodox but still genuine faith. Nicholas Buccola's edited volume
Abraham Lincoln and Liberal Democracy (University Press of Kansas,
2016) contains many excellent essays on Lincoln's thought, including
Steven B. Smith's essay, referenced above, on Lincoln as a Kantian. Diana
Schaub's essay "Lincoln and 'The Public Estimate of the Negro': From
Anti-Amalgamation to Antislavery," which traces Lincoln's attempts to
elevate public opinion toward African Americans, is among the many
excellent entries in Alan Levine, Thomas W. Merrill, and James R. Stoner,
Jr.'s *The Political Thought of the Civil War* (University Press of Kansas, 2018).
Kirk's *The Roots of American Order* (Intercollegiate Studies Institute, 2003)
contains an excellent analysis of Lincoln as a statesman, while Richard
M. Weaver's *The Ethics of Rhetoric*, available from multiple publishers,
contains the most direct comparison of Lincoln and Burke of which I
am aware. It bears special attention for this reason, and its admiration of
Lincoln is a credit to Weaver, a Southerner. Nonetheless, I fear his por-
trait of Lincoln is too doctrinaire and his image of Burke is too flexible.
Prudence, as in all things, must navigate between those positions.

Index